GW00992898

ry
Xmas
1983
Love
is tough!
Jody

TOUGHING IT OUT AT HARVA

TOUGHING IT OUT AT HARVARD

THE MAKING OF A WOMAN MBA

Fran Worden Henry

G. P. Putnam's Sons
New York

Published on the same day in Canada
by General Publishing Co. Limited, Toronto.

Library of Congress Cataloging in Publication Data

Henry, Fran Worden.
Toughing it out at Harvard.

1. Henry, Fran Worden. 2. Harvard University.
Graduate School of Business Administration—Biography.
3. Master of business administration degree—United
States. I. Title.
HF1134.H4H46 1983 650'.092'4 [B] 82-24093
ISBN 0-399-12799-2

PRINTED IN THE UNITED STATES OF AMERICA

Dedication

This book is dedicated to the
struggle for women's equality,
without which I would have had
many fewer opportunities to grow.

CONTENTS

Preface 9

1 Shock Treatment 13

2 Digging In 56

3 Sinking 88

4 Changes 119

5 Playing the Game 144

6 Toughing It Out 174

7 Coasting and Crashing 200

8 Career Choices 221

9 Graduation and Afterthoughts 242

PREFACE

I sat down to write this book on a dare, a dare to myself to say exactly how I felt about spending two years earning an MBA at the Harvard Graduate School of Business Administration. The idea was not mine—it sprang from the foresight of the editorial staff of G. P. Putnam's Sons, who understand the conflicts that many people face as they prepare themselves for tomorrow's careers.

Conflicts abound in my story, and having written it, I wish I could say that this anecdote or that chapter weren't true. But it is true, and for that reason names and backgrounds have been changed to allow my colleagues their privacy.

There is another overriding reason why I was enthusiastic about writing this book. It is because I believe that women must be in top management and corporate boardrooms. We must be there because the business decisions made in those elite places affect every day of our lives and we cannot leave those decisions to chance or to someone else's design.

We should occupy boardrooms and executive suites not because of token nods to our equality but because we are fully trained and prepared to take over the responsibilities we have worked so hard to assume. And in order to get the needed experience, we must get ourselves into educational programs and middle-management spots.

An MBA helps, but it does not have to be from Harvard, for there are now hundreds of MBA programs throughout the country, training the nearly sixty thousand students who attended them in 1982. There are other ways to be trained, too. Getting work experience in computer-related fields, in sales, or in production will be valuable to tomorrow's companies—as will the fields of personnel and human relations as North American managers confront productivity and quality-control problems.

Perhaps the most important thing we can do for the long haul, though, is to begin and to be part of a support system to help women in our companies—to take whatever risks are necessary to share our power and help others grow in our path. I have always used the term *woman-to-woman network*, where the goal is to broaden the power base and create a new decision-making process where women and men jointly determine their economic futures.

On that note, I would like to acknowledge my support system:

Dot Worden, who typed the manuscript and whose "familiar intense stare" corrected many errors. Dot is also my mother.

Joyce Freeland, who formed a partnership with me three years ago but who has yet to see me put a solid month into our business.

Ann Kennedy, Norma Jane Pierce, Laurie Quick, and Virginia Smith, whose struggles at HBS are now legend.

Members of the class of 1982 and of my section, particularly Jane Beule, Phil Catchings, Greg Gorden, Steve Weyl, Betsey Whitbeck, and Gail Williams, and my professors and instructors, particularly Judith Beth Cohen.

Virginia Allan, William and Scott Ferguson, Margie Fisher, Jane Gilley, Chris Miller, Susan Rubin, Joanne Rumrill, Reva Seybolt, Kathy Sreedhar, Sheryl Swed, B. J. Trincilla, and members of my family, who thought I disappeared for two years.

Linda Nelson, Chris Schillig, and Charlotte Sheedy, whose professionalism guided this project to its completion.

Margie Adam, Barbara Price, my role models anear.

Pat Cloherty, Gloria Steinem, my role models afar.

Thank you.

1

SHOCK TREATMENT

It wouldn't have been so bad if that broad-shouldered man hadn't been looking right over my shoulder at the dryer. I was embarrassed when he asked if he could show me how to use it, but I surely needed some kind of help. I had just put my dirty clothes into the dryer, cleaned out the lint, and thrown in the wet soap, having mistaken the dryer for the washer! My hot, sticky clothes circled slowly in front of me, reminding me that I was losing control.

It was Saturday morning. I had finished one week at Harvard Business School, and I was in shock. That very morning I had jumped out of bed at six, forgetting it wasn't a school day. I heated water for my coffee but forgot to put the grounds in a Melitta filter; I tasted a mouthful of grit and was too numb to care.

Terror had hold of me. It had started the evening before the first day of school. First-year students at Harvard Business School (called "first years") registered in Aldrich, the red brick classroom building that would become a second home. We were led from room to room, patiently waiting to get bills paid, identification cards, and student numbers. I chatted with people casually. It was an easygoing time and people looked tanned and rested from the summertime.

The last stop in the process was Baker 20. Baker is the library at Harvard Business School, the biggest building on campus, and it beautifully dominates the landscape. Baker 20 is in the basement of the library and it is where the cases are handed out.

Cases are the foundation of education at the B School. They are usually twenty to forty pages long and in each case a business problem is presented through a description of a company's product, management, or finances. The written description is complemented by pages of graphs and tables. Each student is expected to read and analyze a case and prepare a presentation for class.

I approached the door to Baker 20 and heard nervous laughter from students who had gotten their cases. I couldn't believe it. Each stack of cases was two feet high and everyone was groaning under the load. I cowered at the thought that we were expected to read all the cases I was dragging to my dorm, but a second-year student who heard me complain noted, with some glee, that the stack was only a third of what we would get by year's end.

Back in my dorm room I started to review the material. I read the background on the business school and the *Academic Standards Bulletin.* I read about the health and athletic programs and warnings about rape and burglary. It scared me to think I might not be safe in school buildings.

Then I looked at my cases. First years had no choice in picking courses. For the first four months of school, I had

Production and Operations Management; Marketing; Control; Organizational Behavior; Management Communications; and Managerial Economics. I carefully stacked up all my cases and labeled the piles: POM, MTG, CTL, OB, MC, and ME. I didn't know that those letters would soon dance in my head and creep into my dreams.

But on that warm Tuesday evening, the second of September, 1980, it didn't seem to be too much. After all, we did cases one at a time. I went off unharried to dinner at Kresge Hall, the school cafeteria, and sat with a few students I had met earlier that day. Michael Mitchell was among them; he was a man I had met at registration, when we had discovered we would both be in Section D. Michael was tall and lanky with curly black hair and a very soft smile. I was pleased to join the discussion.

"Well, what did you think about Smucker?" Michael asked.

"Smucker?" I said. "It's all right, I guess. I really don't think about Smucker that much."

"No, not the jam. The case. The Marketing case for tomorrow. What did you think about their strategy for ketchup?"

I couldn't believe the dinner conversation. Just a few hours earlier these men had been full of talk about Boston, about girlfriends. Now they were talking about cases. I scrambled up Kresge steps, hurried over to my dorm room in Chase Hall and pulled out my assignment sheet. Sure enough, the very first class tomorrow—Smucker for Marketing. And there was no indication of what to do. The only hint was the terse line: "Prepare J. M. Smucker Company."

One and a half hours later I bit a fingernail. I was starting to get nervous. I didn't know what Smucker was *trying* to do, no less what it *should* do. It was eight o'clock and I thought

I'd better read my other cases. I turned to Control, Harvard's word for management accounting. At least this professor had the good manners to give an assignment. It read:

> Power Mowers, Inc.
> 1. Complete the cash flow forecast for 1967.
> 2. Complete a *pro forma* income statement.
> 3. If the bank won't extend credit, what should Mr. Harmon do?

I read Power Mowers twice— it wasn't very long. Somehow I expected to read about how to do a cash flow and income statement, but there were no clues in the case. There was no clue either about why a bank loans money to people like Mr. Harmon, the owner of Power Mowers.

It was 9:30 and very hot in my room. I threw open the window by my desk and in came a rush of cool air, although I was too agitated to appreciate the breeze.

Just then I heard a voice, loud and sure, from the courtyard below. "There are no answers. There are *no* answers."

He must have been a second-year student and past the frustration I felt at that moment.

This must be a joke. How can I be rattled when I've only been studying a few hours? Sure, I knew people were expected to talk in class. I knew that someone was called on in each class to "open" the case. But I also knew there were eighty-seven students in my class. Why was I panicked about not knowing how to do a cash flow forecast? And what was I doing here if I didn't know how to do the first assignment?

What was I doing here? At thirty-two, I had been out of school for ten years. My résumé was chock-full of challenging work. Since high school I had set goals for myself and savored their achievement. When my parents couldn't afford the tuition and board to send me to college, I found work and, along with loans and scholarships, paid my way through school. When I had completed three years toward my bachelor's degree in psychology, I became dissatisfied with my education and applied to and was accepted into a two-year program at the New School for Social Research in New York City.

I was headed for a career in psychology, and in order to get my degree at the New School, I designed a program which required that I work for a year in the admitting office of Bellevue Psychiatric Hospital. I was very committed to meshing public service with my career goals, for I was one of those young people fired up by John Kennedy in his 1961 inaugural address when he asked Americans to contribute to their country. Although I was only twelve when I heard his words, I recalled them clearly as I set out in 1971 with my B.A. in social science.

My B.A. trained me to work with people, but my experience at Bellevue tarnished my desire to be a psychologist. At nineteen I found myself confronted each day with dozens of seriously ill people and I wanted more than anything to change their lives. I became frustrated with the slow pace of mental health healing and decided that I would be happier if I could use my sensitivities more directly in dealing with people in some management capacity.

A stroke of luck got me a job as the executive director of the Massachusetts Commission on the Status of Women, which served Governor Frank Sargent. Sargent was a liberal Republican committed to bringing young people into state government and to changing discriminatory laws against women. After a few years of working in state government, though, I wanted to work at national and international levels and to see what the government was like in Washington, D.C.

Once there, I worked again in the women's movement, as the acting director of a presidential committee for women under Gerald Ford and then for President Carter's International Women's Year Commission, headed by Bella Abzug. In two and a half years, the commission and staff helped organize and lead fifty-five state and territorial meetings and a huge national women's conference in Houston.

When the conference was over, I wanted to work outside the United States and joined the staff of an emerging publicly funded company, A. T. International. As director of communications for ATI, I helped set in motion a firm whose purpose is to help small business and community groups in developing countries. In the process I traveled through Asia, Africa, and Latin America and had a chance to see and understand the position of women in industrializing countries.

In the midst of the trail I had blazed for myself, I became acutely aware of my deficiencies. When someone asked me to draw up a budget, my mind went immediately blank. As a senior staffer at ATI, when I was furnished with financial statements, my eyes glazed over the items listed on the income statement and balance sheet. Worse still, I feared that even though I had proven myself over and over in various jobs, in a new position I would always have to prove myself again. I could see my career in government limited to project management and the thought of it made me restless. I began to think about starting a business of my own, but at thirty, with no business training, I was reluctant to take the risk.

Business school seemed like the answer. A decade ago, when I was married and living in Cambridge, I had looked at Harvard University with deference. At the time I was supporting my husband while he studied at Harvard Graduate

School of Design, and I remember I often watched students hurry across Anderson Bridge to the Harvard Business School. I wistfully dreamed about going to such a place—with power emanating from the red brick, ivy, and gold cupolas across the Charles River. To outsiders, the B School was a mysterious place. When we talked about it, or if we knew someone who went there, a sense of awe was invoked, as though the school were the seat of success, a giant Wizard of Oz in the business world. I decided to apply.

Once I set the wheels in motion, I put a lot of energy into my decision. I chose to apply to Stanford and Harvard because, in terms of quality of education, these schools were rated numbers one and two by business educators. I applied to only two schools because I knew it would take a lot of time to learn about and visit each one, and with a full-time job, I could only handle two choices.

Stanford was gorgeous to see and had a comfortable class size of three hundred fifty. The Stanford Business School program stressed the technical side of managing business and gave students quantitative skills in finance, marketing, and production. Harvard's program aimed at teaching general management skills, and the school itself captured my heart when I sat in on classes and talked to professors. There was so much going on in class, so much enthusiasm and participation. It reminded me of my New School classes, where we had studied original works, argued philosophical questions, and steered away from textbooks and pat lectures.

The application process was a nightmare. For weeks I wrote essays deep into the night, and I requested recommendations from people who knew me and my work. Recommendations are very important in most admissions offices, because they are the only way the admissions committee gets a third-party, personal view. I struggled with the question of whom I should turn to and finally risked asking the chairman of the board of a large company who knew me from ATI and was a well-known leader in the women's movement

I realized, too, how important recommendations were, because when my colleague in the women's movement sent me a copy of what she had written to Harvard and Stanford, it made me proud and self-confident to read what she had said about me. It was a special treat to hear later from the admissions office about how important that letter was to at least the female staff in admissions. Apparently they were accustomed to letters from board chairmen, but they hadn't seen many from the women's movement and were thrilled to see my supporter's signature and to know that she, as a woman, could validate and support another woman.

Another requirement of my candidacy was to take the General Management Admissions Test. It was unnerving to sit in a crowded classroom and take a test with people five and ten years younger than I was. I didn't get the gist of a lot of the test and my score reflected it: right in the middle range. I hoped my other qualifications would give me a chance at being admitted.

When I was accepted by both schools, I registered a moment of shaky insecurity. I wondered what was wrong with their admissions process that they had accepted me. But soon I settled down and focused on my choices. Advice from a friend steered me toward Harvard. She said that although Stanford training is top-notch, the people from big business who recruit and hire are Harvard alumni and are more likely to look on a Harvard graduate with favor. It was also easy to choose Harvard because it fit better into my career goals. I had just started a small business advisory service with Joyce Freeland, a CPA, and we wanted to provide financial and marketing counseling in the Northeast. In New England, a Harvard degree would mean more than one from Stanford.

But when it came right down to it, it was the school itself I wanted. Harvard Business School, nearly seventy-five years old, had a history and reputation that seemed to equal the best of American business. While I knew it might reflect the worst in American business too, I was confident that being past thirty, my values were well in place and I would not lose myself in the process of getting my degree.

It was awesome to learn about the school. Harvard accepted seven hundred fifty students a year from the eight thousand who applied. We enrolled in a two-year, full-time program which allowed, according to the admissions brochure, no time for part-time anything. We were expected to work during the summer between out first and second years and report to the school on our experiences. Our education would cost roughly twenty-five thousand dollars, a sum that included an estimation of living expenses.

The faculty numbered one hundred eighty and they were highly trained people, some of them famous for their research work. Most, however, seemed to have distinguished themselves by their ability to teach the case method. Successful faculty members could lead a case discussion like a conductor a symphony orchestra. And the case method was the primary pedagogical tool. From my observations and reading, its purpose was to teach students through a lifelike grappling with facts—it forced us to make decisions in our preparation for class and forced us to act like managers once in class. The eighty-minute-long classes were comprised almost totally of student discussion, and it took a very skilled professor to pull concepts and solid learning out of the jumble that ensued.

I liked the intellectual challenge of it, but it was not just that which made me apply to and then choose Harvard. It was the excitement of doing something in a man's domain which I wasn't sure I could do. And it was the need to satisfy my curiosity about what made business and economics tick. Yet that wasn't really it. Way down deep I knew why I was at Harvard and why I'd do my best to stay.

It was power. Power to know how to make things happen. Power to make choices, power to be independent, power to be heard and show how I feel. Plain old power.

Summoning my thoughts back to my dorm room and taking a deep breath, I focused again on Power Mowers, Inc. I dug out *Accounting Principles*, the reference text I had bought that day, hoping it had some mention of cash flow statements. Unfortunately it had whole chapters on the subject, and by the time I'd read through them and questioned my roommate and a couple of men down the hall, I was thoroughly confused. I scribbled some notes about the value of cash flow in predicting the need for money and moved on to my next case.

It was 11 P.M. It struck me that I had three classes every day and three cases every night. Fifteen classes, fifteen cases every week. When would I have time to call my friends, my business partner, my family?

My next case was for the Organizational Behavior class, and looking at it gave me some relief. This course will be about people, I thought, and I might have a chance to understand it. The case was Robert F. Kennedy High School; we were expected to take the principal's position and help solve his problems in managing student-faculty confrontations. The assignment directed me to prepare a "time-phased action plan." By 12:30 I had worked out a program of sorts, although I was too worn out to care if it had any cohesion.

Earlier in the evening my goal had been to jog and relax

before going to sleep, but I fell into my bed exhausted. Although the next morning was warm and sunny, I knew summer was over. School had begun.

Only two people were in Aldrich 12 when I opened the door to Section D's classroom. It was early, 8 A.M., and though class did not begin until 8:30, a few of us were there to stake a claim to a favorite seat.

There were seven hundred eighty-five students in the class of 1982, more than the norm. The registrar's office had divided us into nine sections, each one a class of eighty-five or so students. The school took great care, we were informed, to make each section a balanced group of students in terms of age, experience, industry background, gender, race, nationality, and technical training. The mix of many points of view in a section contributed to the richness of class discussion, and it was one of the elements of our education about which the school seemed most proud.

The sections were lettered A through I; I was assigned to Section D. Students stayed with the same section, the same students and professors, and the same classroom for the entire year. Each day, Monday through Friday, we had three classes, at 8:30, 10:10, and 1:00. Our six professors and courses alternated days and times.

We had a different professor for each course, and we had no choice about whom we would get. On registration day there had been a lot of speculation about professors, but I came across few people who had heard of mine and it seemed that second-year students felt more identity with "old Section D" than with professors. I looked forward to meeting my instructors face to face. On the first day I would have Marketing and meet Thomas Rhinehart, then Organizational Behavior with Bob Murphy, and Control with Kirk Cranston. Later in the week or early the next week, there would be Production and Operations Management with Duke Moore, Management Communications with Margaret Price, and Managerial Economics with Joseph Horst.

All of the sections had classes in Aldrich, a large brick building next to Baker Library. The classrooms looked alike too. Section D's was a windowless amphitheater. There were six rows of seats in semicircles. The walls were dull pink, the floors a red linoleum. Bright green blackboards dominated the front of the room. Seats were the hardwood kind, and though they were attached to the floor, they swiveled and bent back. I didn't realize how important these minor movements were; they would be the only ones permitted during our eighty-minute classes.

I had heard about classroom seating strategy at registration the day before. The top row of seats was called the skydeck. People who sat there didn't want to be too involved in discussion, or wanted to be free to read the morning paper or eat lunch early. The bottom row of seats was called the pit. The pit belonged to the professors. If a student sat there, he or she couldn't get away with much except looking down and taking notes.

The "heavies" sat in the center section of the room. Those students got to stare straight down at the professor and look him in the eye when he got too close. The sides of the room were comfortable safety zones. Apparently it was important to pick the right spot because we were expected to stay in one place while each professor memorized our faces and names. I realized that this system, with the teachers changing classes while the students stayed put, was the same as that in my junior high school. The rigidity of it made me feel claustrophobic.

I took a seat in the third row on the right side of the room and, along with everyone else, put my name card in the slot in front of me. Our common names or nicknames were printed meticulously with black letters on the front and back of heavy white posterboard. A solid feeling of belonging came with the card; it felt like a badge of honor, and I was proud to sit behind it.

I studied my classmates filing in, most of whom seemed happy enough to be here. Some shook their heads and started talking about the day's cases. Most hoped someone else would be called on. Nearly everyone was dressed neatly, wearing khaki pants, leather belts, Izod shirts, and loafers. A few women wore sundresses and cotton sweaters. My classmates carried a clean-cut, establishment look and met my expectations of what a Harvard class would look like. What surprised me was my sense of age in response to their youth. Being over thirty had never seemed that old to me, but being surrounded with twenty-five-year-olds made me feel somehow cautious.

I had some reason to be cautious. Students at Harvard were among the top business students in the country, according to opinions of faculty and employers. My colleagues were known for their quick, aggressive intelligence and their potential for being future chief executive officers of the world's largest companies. We each got a copy of Section D student résumés, and looking through them caused me to have some thoughts about whether I belonged there. It looked like there wasn't a slouch among us.

Take George Cohen for starters. He had already gotten a graduate degree in computer science from MIT and had an undergraduate degree in mathematics. His work experience included computer operations at Citibank.

And Irene Lenkowski. She had a bachelor's degree in math from Smith College and had held a top position at IBM before leaving to come back to school at age thirty-six. My roommate, Pat Worth, knew three languages, was a Phi Beta Kappa linguistics graduate, and had already completed a two-year financial analyst training program at Chase Manhattan Bank. Another female student, Sheryl Shaw, was educated as a chemist and had worked for du Pont de Nemours in specialty fabric applications.

Another résumé caught my eye. It was that of Alan Talmadge, a graduate of Harvard a few years ago with a B.A. in population studies. He had worked in theater in New York before coming to school, and he obviously had an interest in the arts. Another "humanist" type was Kate McRae, whose résumé showed her to be more like me than anyone I'd seen thus far. She had an undergraduate degree in English from the University of Chicago and had managed political campaigns in Georgia and an experimental artists' group before leaving for B School.

The book went on, page after page. I saw that Michael Mitchell had a bachelor's degree in engineering and six years of management experience with A.T.&T. I couldn't help but be struck by the number of men from the military. Quite a few had gone from West Point or Annapolis to significant military duty and now were at school. There were a number of people from other countries: Malaysia, Ecuador, France, Britain, India, Japan, Germany, and Switzerland. These students had equally outstanding backgrounds: one student was an Olympic skier and another an OPEC negotiator for his country. The patchwork pattern of everyone's experience and qualifications made a very impressive whole. There seemed to be people from every conceivable industry. When I looked up the class statistics in the school handbook, I was even more impressed, though I also felt some anxiety.

About seventy-five percent of the class had quantitative

backgrounds, with degrees in economics, engineering, and science. Nearly one-quarter already had graduate degrees. The class was heavily weighed toward younger people; eighty-two percent were twenty-three to twenty-eight years old. Only fourteen percent were in my bracket, twenty-nine or over. Thirty percent were married. Twenty-one percent of the class were international students; only nine percent were from racial minorities. And twenty-four percent of the seven hundred eighty-five students in the class of 1982 were women.

As I looked around the room, I wondered whether the students who surrounded me were there for reasons like mine. Or did their youth and education make them different, perhaps more in tune with the career paths that Harvard's placement office would lay out for them? I didn't have much time to wonder because it was one minute to 8:30.

The classroom had buzzed with the movement of books, people, and squeaking seats but it abruptly came to an end. Silence ushered in our first professor: Thomas Rhinehart, Assistant Professor, Marketing.

No one seemed to have heard about Thomas Rhinehart. Apparently he had been teaching at Harvard for one year; I overheard someone say he had a Ph.D. in English, and I wondered why he was at HBS teaching Marketing.

The course was designed to provide us with the basic analytical tools needed to develop marketing strategy. Segments of the course, according to the curriculum, include the marketing process; product planning and market selection; communications; distribution; marketing research; and pricing.

Professor Rhinehart arranged his papers at the front of the room. Then he spoke right up. His introduction was brief; he told us to call him Thomas. He welcomed us to the Harvard Business School and briefly lectured on Harvard as a proud tradition. I wondered why he told us that we deserved each other's respect in the classroom. And then, with no further fanfare, he asked us to consider J. M. Smucker Co.

"Should they introduce ketchup to the marketplace, and if so, how should they do it?" Thomas said. "Stan Hooper, I thought we'd ask you to tell the class your opinion."

Everyone in the room swallowed hard. That morning I wouldn't have been able to describe the ten seconds that followed a classmate being called on. But after many similar moments in later classes I realized what was happening because the drama unfolded in the same way every day. Each one of us knew we might be called on, but very few of us thought we had prepared well enough to present our analysis and conclusions to the class. When one of us was called on, the other eighty-six closed our eyes briefly, gave thanks to whomever we believed in, and tried not to let our relief and state of grace show. Our anxiety was collectively suspended in the cool air of the classroom.

It seemed like an hour before Stan started to speak. When he did, everyone in the classroom started to move. We weren't nailed; now we were free to support Stan and we did, hoping he had read the case and would be able to talk about it.

I watched him closely and wondered what was going through his mind. He was one of the men who had been trained at West Point and I wondered if he'd had similar classroom experiences there. He spoke up, though he looked like he was operating on pure adrenaline and not really in control of what he said.

"Smucker is a company which produces jam. They had sales of fifteen point eight million dollars in nineteen sixty-seven, the time of the case. They sell jam to retail stores under their own label."

He spoke for ten minutes or so, mostly recalling what we had read in the case. He listed Smucker's options very concisely, but he didn't draw any conclusions. I was stunned by him because sitting there simply watching Stan Hooper talk made me so nervous that I couldn't remember any of Smucker's options or any of the case facts he seemed to cite so readily.

Stan ended his opening, our first Section D cold-call, saying "Well, I guess that's all."

A dozen hands shot up, and Thomas recognized one, a student who sat two seats away from me. I could hear his heavy breathing as he told us how Smucker should branch out and sell ketchup through a private label. He thought Heinz and Del Monte were too big to compete with. How did he know that, I wondered?

I didn't have time to think about his comment, though, for we were on to another student. And it was an entirely different point. George Cohen was talking about the harm he saw to its jam business if Smucker were to sell ketchup.

The next hour rushed by, a whirl of comments that had no beginning and no end. Thomas stopped the class by asking us a dozen questions which we had no capacity to understand.

"Consider this," he said. "Is the price right for the eight-ounce size? Will the consumer pay for it? What is the margin for the grocer and how does it compare to the margin he or she gets from Heinz or Del Monte? Can Smucker sell a staple item when they usually sell jam, an impulse purchase? Can Smucker transfer its advertising image from jam ' like Mother used to make ' to ketchup? Do consumers think mothers ever made ketchup?"

Well there was no right answer, it seemed, but I did get the feeling that ketchup was a bad move for J. M. Smucker Co.

Class was over after a short statement by Thomas. He said,

"Please be prepared to open every day. If you are not prepared to open or if you cannot come to class, please call me before class begins. Missing class without an excuse is counted against you. Do not repeat case facts in your opening; present an analysis of the case material which led to your decision. You must tell the class what you decided and why. Your presentation should take ten to fifteen minutes and serve as the agenda for the rest of the discussion. Thank you. Class dismissed."

Everyone burst out of their seats, relieved to have the class over. A number of students clapped Stan on the back, congratulating him, but Stan thought he had done poorly and cited Rhinehart's lecture at the close of class as a condemnation of his opening. No one could console him.

We had a twenty-minute break before the next class, time enough to run to the bathroom and catch my breath. There were five stalls and fifteen women waiting to go. Apparently the first- and second-year classes let out at the same time and there was one bathroom per floor for the three hundred seventy-five women who had to use the facilities. Kate, a woman from my section, looked at me, smiled, and said, "Even when we get relief, there's no relief."

I laughed and smiled back. Kate McRae might become a friend, I thought. I had met her at registration, when we found out we'd both be in the same section. She was a very striking person: tall, with long, curly hair, wide-set eyes, and she had a strong, athlete's body. When I asked about her family, she told me that her husband, Todd, lived at their home in Houston and practiced law. Kate planned to go home every other weekend and hoped school would fit into her schedule.

On registration day we laughed about our backgrounds. Kate had seen the résumé book too and picked out the few of us who had liberal arts training. When she showed the book to her husband, he leafed through it silently. Then he looked up and cheered Kate with the observation, "Well, it looks like you're the spice."

She, like me, was there to get some credibility in a world stacked against women. She was tired of working hard but not being taken seriously as a career person. We wondered aloud if our "no-numbers" education would get in our way. As we walked back to class, we decided to meet Friday night and talk more about why we were here at business school.

Back in our classroom, we were seated by 10:10 precisely. Organizational Behavior was about to start. This course was aimed at giving students a grounding in human aspects of management. With a better understanding of human behavior we were more likely to be able to influence people. The course included sections on group behavior; individual behavior; motivation; leadership; designing complex organizations; and managing change. We were expected to learn conflict management; interpersonal behavior; managing subordinates; giving and receiving feedback; performance appraisal, reward incentive systems; and action planning.

Our professor, Bob Murphy, walked into the room. Like Rhinehart, he wasn't known to any of us by reputation, but he was an older man who had graduated from HBS many years before and had been teaching at the school since then. Later I learned that few HBS professors were well known in their fields, the way, for example, that Harvard Law School professors were known. This was apparently true because case research was important in developing an instructor into a professor, and case research was a rather private pursuit inside businesses, not something likely to bring fame and public praise. I hoped that Bob Murphy would be an experienced and giving person because I knew that OB was a course I could enjoy if the tone in the classroom were right.

He started the class with a nod of his head and called on Alan Talmadge to come down to the front of the room. Alan was to sit in a chair and role-play the principal of Robert F. Kennedy High School. He was instructed to tell us what he would do with dissident high school students, and we were directed to respond.

Alan was a big man, built like a football hero. I wondered if he had been called on because of his work in the theater. Bob Murphy could have assumed he was familiar with audiences. His eyes were clear and very bright as he moved toward the chair, but once there he hunched himself up as though one of us would shoot arrows at him.

The professor stood in back of him and waited for Alan to finish talking, and when he did, Bob clipped him on the back and said, "Congratulations, Alan, that is the most attention you may ever need to suffer at Harvard Business School."

Was that true? In just two classes I had seen men called on to talk in front of the class while we were encouraged to tear apart their contributions. And if this was a warm-up, what would a regular class be like?

I watched Bob Murphy closely. It seemed as if he called on anyone who put his or her hand up and he had no control over what that person said. Every comment took off in another direction. When Alan was in front of the room and spoke as the principal of the school, he thought he could help student unrest if he met with the students. As he spoke he outlined a plan for doing it. But the comments that followed suggested other strategies: some people thought the teachers should handle the conflict and the principal should stay out of it; one student thought the students should be given rules and be expected to follow them. There was no consensus and

Bob Murphy summed up the class by saying that there were a lot of ways to look at conflict—further cases would help us design strategies for dealing with it.

Class was dismissed; I had finished two classes and had one to go in order to finish my first day at school. My schedule allowed an hour and a half for lunch and it whizzed by as I did errands. I found it easy to maneuver on campus. Harvard Business School is located on sixty-one acres on the Boston side of the Charles River. The B School, as it is commonly called, is physically separate from the rest of the university and maintains a commanding presence with the broad red buildings and Georgian architecture.

The faculty and administration planned a tight-knit community. On campus students can get food, laundry, and dry-cleaning services, haircuts, and use a travel agency. We can buy all of our books and supplies, cash checks, and go to the post office within a few yards of the library. We also enjoy use of the athletic facilities—basketball, tennis, and squash courts, a swimming pool, indoor and outdoor tracks, and a hockey rink—within a block of classrooms.

As I hurried through the maze of buildings, I spotted some section mates moving toward Aldrich. Sarah Ann Collins, a woman who sat across the room from me, was in the group, as well as Michael Mitchell, my dinner companion from the previous night. I joined them and overheard their conversation about the morning's class. I remembered Sarah Ann from the résumé book; she had a B.S. with honors in computer science and was from the South.

"What did Thomas mean in Marketing?" Sarah Ann said. "He wants analysis in our opening statements, not case facts, but how do we do that?"

"I don't know, Sarah Ann," Michael said, "but at lunch I ran into a second-year student who had Rhinehart last year and he said he didn't know any more about what Thomas wanted on the final day of class than he did on the first."

"How about Control?" I asked.

Control was our next class. We each pulled out our work sheets and the income statements we had done the night before. Each of us had arrived at a different figure for net income, but class began in a minute and we had no time to redo our work.

Kirk Cranston was our Control instructor. I was surprised when I looked at him; he was clearly five or six years younger than I was. He described himself as an Australian, a graduate of the B School the previous spring. He was also a certified public accountant and while at school had been a Baker Scholar.

Baker Scholar was a distinction reserved for the top five percent of the graduating class of Harvard Business School. The distinction implied that a student had gotten excellent grades in most of his courses. Kirk seemed so cheerful, so self-confident as he strode around the front of the classroom with his blue three-piece suit. He seemed fully capable of teaching us Control, the course that had made me so agitated the night before, when I had tried to do the case.

Control was a course designed to provide students with a thorough understanding of the flow of money through a company. The course included segments on accounting systems; financial statements; the external financial reporting process; cost accounting systems; and management control procedures. It sounded dense and was exactly what I had come to school to learn.

After introducing himself, Kirk started the class discussion with a description of Power Motors. "What are the problems of companies which are growing fast?" he asked.

A few students raised their hands, and when called on,

they actually answered. They knew why companies had problems; they seemed to know what inventory was and just how it sucked cash away from other operations. The students who answered Kirk's questions seemed to know so much about companies like Power Mowers that I wondered why they were in school at all. I sat mesmerized listening to my colleagues and thinking about their backgrounds and how smart they seemed to be.

Finally it was 2:30 and class was dismissed. I had the whole afternoon to myself, so I packed up my swimming gear and went to the pool. I pounded the water, swimming much harder than I usually did, swimming out the tensions of the day. A whole night and day had gone by and I hadn't learned very much. I had been quiet all day. I hadn't even raised my hand.

I knew Kate felt the same way. She met me after my swim and walked me to my dorm. We were both unnerved by the fast pace of the discussions. And some students didn't seem bothered by talking: Stan Hooper had talked in every class and seemed pleased with himself by the end of the day. Pat Worth had seemed comfortable in Control; she had answered Kirk's questions more than once. I felt uneasy about not talking, even though it was the first day of school. I didn't want to get into a rut and I knew class participation was important to my grade.

By 4 P.M. I had showered and was thinking about reading the paper, but when I settled down, instead of relaxing, I felt a gripping uneasiness in my stomach. I'd better do a case.

Pulling out the assignment sheet, I noticed we had Marketing and Control cases and Managerial Economics for the next day. I looked the cases over. It was impossible to know where to begin, so I picked Marketing.

We were assigned Butcher Polish Company, along with

notes on breakeven analysis and marketing arithmetic. I read the breakeven note but didn't understand one thing it said. Then I read about marketing arithmetic. I listed the terms we were supposed to understand, terms like *profit margin, fixed cost, overhead.* We needed to put numbers to these terms in order to do a breakeven. Well, what was a breakeven for?

Maybe if I read Butcher Polish it would be clear. I remembered one of the professors earlier in the day encouraging us to think beyond the case to the meaning and purpose of it. If we could figure it out, then we'd save ourselves a lot of time scrambling down other, unrelated, paths of thinking. I assumed Butcher Polish was about breakeven analysis.

According to the first line of the case, the key question for Butcher Polish Company, manufacturer of floor wax, was whether their selling approach was correct. Did that relate to breakeven? I had no clue and read on. I took notes for two hours but still didn't come to a conclusion. Then I reread the notes, trying to find numbers in the case that would match up to the terms I was supposed to learn. Nothing matched. Pat came back from dinner and reminded me the cafeteria closed in fifteen minutes. It was quarter to seven, and I had better get down there if I intended to eat.

At dinner, I joined Sarah Ann and George Cohen from Section D and a student I hadn't met before. They were complaining about the food when I sat down (apparently the salad bar was much more expensive than they thought it should be), and I interrupted them to ask if anyone had done Butcher Polish. It didn't matter to me that just last night I had criticized my companions for talking about Marketing at dinner—I was desperate.

Neither Sarah Ann nor George had done Butcher Polish—they had worked on Freemark Abbey Winery for Managerial Economics. But another fellow at the table had.

"What about breakeven analysis?" I said.

"That's not the point," he replied. "You should look instead at what the competition, Beacon Wax, is doing."

As I got up to leave I mumbled thanks, but realized when I got back to my room that I hadn't even asked his name. How rude of me, I thought; this isn't like me. I wanted to dig into Butcher Polish again, but it was late and instead I had to move on.

By 9:30 I had read and taken notes on Freemark Abbey Winery. Just looking at the Managerial Economics cases made me jumpy and now I knew why.

Managerial Economics was probably going to be my hardest course, because its very description was like a foreign language to me. Its aim was to give students techniques for making decisions based on numbers. To do that we were going to learn how to assess risk, how to forecast, how to analyze the time value of cash flows, and how to work with computers by doing regression analysis and linear programming.

With Freemark Abbey Winery we were apparently looking at uncertainty, for given the likelihood of a thunderstorm, we were supposed to decide whether or not to harvest ripe grapes in a vineyard. Different probabilities of financial success or failure were associated with the vineyard's options. No matter which way I organized my notes, I didn't come to any conclusion. If Freemark Abbey harvested right away, I reasoned, it would be the safest course, even though I could not say how much money they would earn or what quality wine would be produced. I knew we were expected to be more precise than that. What was the secret? I didn't have time to figure it out, because the Control case waited to be done.

I thought I was lucky with Control because we were assigned Power Mowers, the same case we had done today. But tonight we were expected to complete a balance sheet and funds flow statement and predict Mr. Harmon's monthly need for cash. Oh my God, I thought. I should have done this first. It's 10:45, my eyes are bleary, my head actually hurts, and I have rarely seen a balance sheet. How can I do one?

I cried out to Pat and she appeared like an angel, balance sheet in hand. Pat Worth was my assigned roommate. She seemed to be a nice person, although both of us had kept our distance for the first few days since we had moved into Chase Hall. We were also assigned to the same section by some random action of the computer, which made it inevitable that we'd spend a lot of time together. Pat was twenty-eight and accustomed to her own place in New York City. I was used to my own place, too. Both of us had requested single rooms, but dormitory space was tight and most students were doubled up.

Pat and I had particularly troublesome space. We each had a room with sickly green walls and brown tile floors. Pat's was six feet by ten feet and mine was twelve feet by ten feet. The room was originally designed to be a bedroom and study for one person, so Pat had to cross through my room in order to get to the outside hall and bathroom. Neither of us had privacy, but we took dorm rooms rather than renting apartments because we wanted to be close to campus and the help of nearby students. I felt I'd been out of school too long to study by myself. We tried to make the best of our situation, stepping around one another and being as polite as we could.

Right at that moment I was so grateful for her standing there in her pajamas and robe holding out her balance sheet. It looked so good as I copied it down: assets, liabilities, and retained earnings. I didn't understand where the numbers came from, and Pat tried to explain. She said that before she had come to Harvard, she had worked for Chase Manhattan Bank in New York doing financial analysis, and the bank training course she had attended was taught by a Harvard professor.

"Balance sheets," Pat said, "are simply a statement of what a company owns and owes for a point in time. On the assets side, you'd find all of the things of value—cash or money in the bank; inventory, that's the unsold product; land; buildings; and accounts receivable—the money owed by people who have bought the product. On the liabilities side, you'd find everything that the company owes to people, like unpaid wages, trade credit, bank loans.

"The difference between assets and liabilities," she went on to say, "is net worth, or what belongs to the stockholders, who own the corporation."

I know it sounded simple, and Pat looked at me very patiently, but I couldn't get it. How could anyone at one point in time know all of those things? And what did stockholders own, the cash part or the land part of the assets? I remembered Control class and Kirk's warning to us. He was willing to help us out, he said, if we worked hard. But we weren't supposed to come to him with questions if they could have been answered by the green book—a multiple-choice workbook sent to first-year students over the summer. It was meant to serve as an introduction to basic accounting, and if we completed it, we were supposedly ready for the first cases. But we were into subjects much more complex than the green book and I was lost.

Funds flow was next and it was midnight. Funds flow was the third in the trio of important financial statements—balance sheets and income statements being the other two.

Funds flow was the statement that showed how money came into and went out of a company. But I had no idea how to draw up the format or what contents should be in the statement, and it was getting late. Usually I went to bed by at least 11 o'clock, and two nights in a row I had gone past my limit.

I closed my eyes and the fear of not knowing how to do my work overwhelmed me. I started to hallucinate about funds flow. Funds flows were the sea; they moved in great waves and swirled around me. Great mountains of money moved toward the ocean then washed back again.

I tried to get a grip on myself by meditating, and I repeated my mantra, a symbol from transcendental meditation that I had learned many years before but hadn't used often. When I took some deep breaths and calmed down, I realized I'd done as much as I could for the night and decided to go to bed. But I lay awake for a long time. Images, numbers, faces, and strange animals started to bounce inside my head, throbbing with a heavy beat. It must have been past two when I drifted off to sleep.

My second day at Harvard Business School inched along minute by minute. In Control, Kirk asked for volunteers who wanted to demonstrate their financial statements. Again, I was surprised to see an income statement and a balance sheet and a funds flow go up on the blackboard. Someone had understood the assignment. Kirk explained that the first two days were introductory, that we shouldn't worry if we didn't understand. The next few weeks, he said, would be spent on the basics of accounting and then we would go back to financial statements.

"Don't worry if you don't get it all," he said. "You'll have more time to spend on the topics we covered yesterday and today."

I found it hard not to worry. In the same statement he told us that the certified public accountants in the room were expected not to participate for three or four weeks, to let the students who didn't know accounting do the talking. That made no sense to me; why should those of us who didn't understand do all the talking?

The next class, Butcher Polish for Marketing, started promptly. Thomas Rhinehart asked Kate to open, and I was amazed because she appeared so composed.

She looked up at Thomas and said, "You may want to call on someone else. I've just found out in study group that I have my breakevens wrong."

"Try as best you can, Kate," Thomas said, which surprised me because he had remarked the day before that we'd better not come to class if we hadn't done our breakeven analysis right.

Kate described the company and its problems. She reviewed their current strategy of selling wax through hardware stores and presented some numbers on the cases of wax that Butcher Polish had to sell to meet its goals. I was impressed. It was the first time she had spoken, and she was prepared. I was ready to give her a wink across the room when a number of students shot up their hands. Thomas recognized a fellow by the name of Richard Travis.

"I thoroughly disagree; the strategy the company employs isn't working," he said.

Where on earth did he come from, I wondered. Why doesn't he say what a great job Kate did? My mind left the classroom and the discussion for a while. I had to think about the whole process. Sitting in class, I felt like I was in the middle of a circus with comments jumping out everywhere. The handful who spoke in the first classes didn't relate to each other's statements. There was no support for anything a student said, and once recognized, people blurted out whatever was on their minds. No one who spoke listened to anyone else; it seemed as if they were just competing to take up air time.

As I focused on the room and the conversation again, I heard students commenting on the money the storekeeper got from a case of wax. It seemed to make a difference how much money the storekeeper got, because it was given a label-dealer margin, and it became clear that the higher it was, the better.

"Why should a hardware store get more than a supermarket?" Thomas asked.

"It shouldn't," a guy in front of me said.

Suddenly I had my hand up in the air. Before I could be sensible and put it down, Thomas called on me.

"Fran?"

Everyone waited as I called up the courage to speak, and I felt a curious sense of power as eighty-six students and Thomas Rhinehart stared at me.

"Well, the customer in the supermarket is different from the customer in the hardware store. My mother usually shops in the supermarket; my father is a carpenter and he goes to the hardware store. The difference between the way they shop may make a difference to Butcher Polish."

I closed my mouth and waited. Thomas looked really happy, but I had no idea why. He asked me to elaborate, but I could only repeat what I'd already said. Thomas called on someone else, but I couldn't listen. I had spoken. I was drained, I was scared, but I had spoken. After many more comments, Thomas summed up the discussion.

"This case," he said, "is about different marketing strategies for products. A product is not a thing. It is a concept, created by the way it is sold to the marketplace. Butcher Polish Company used to sell Butcher Wax in hardware stores. To sell Butcher Wax, the hardware store owner needed to know about the product, and when a customer like Fran's father came into the store, he would tell him that Butcher was the best wax around.

"Now, times have changed. Butcher Polish Company wants to sell its wax in the supermarket. Profit is made on volume sales in supermarkets. Therefore, the company can't expect the supermarket owner to sell Butcher Wax to a customer instead of Beacon or Johnson's Wax. The supermarket is only interested in which one sells the most units, and in order to do that, Butcher Polish must sell to customers, mainly women, through advertising. The customer must want Butcher Wax before he or she comes into the store and only advertising can do that."

It was a great concept, I thought. I had never heard it before and it made a lot of sense. As I got up from my seat, my neighbor, Marsha Dunlop, told me there was a name for what Thomas described. It was called a "push versus pull" strategy. Push vs. pull—a hardware store personal sell vs. a supermarket advertising sell. That was what the case was all about. It disturbed me to realize that I thought the case was about breakevens, and it disturbed me that Marsha knew exactly what it was about when I didn't. How was I ever supposed to know that the case was about a concept I hadn't learned until I got to class?

At lunch I discovered that at least some of the others didn't know either. *Push vs. pull* was a new term for them, too. I also learned the technique I hadn't known the previous night for Freemark Abbey Winery, and with no more thought for Marketing, I started to focus on ME. The vineyard could make a better decision on its grape crop with the aid of a "tree." The tree is a tool which allows a decision maker to lay out all the options on a forked pattern. Decisions which have to be made are labeled "decision forks." A decision fork for Freemark Abbey was whether or not to harvest. Occurrences which take place without decisions are labeled "event forks." An event fork was whether there would be a storm. The probability of an event happening is also labeled; we were given that information in the case when the vineyard owner said that a thunderstorm had a fifty-percent chance of occurring. The financial consequences of events are calculated and then multiplied by the probabilities of the events. At the end of the tree process, the vineyard can isolate the best decision from an economic point of view.

"George, how did you ever know this stuff?" I asked. George Cohen, who sat in front of me in class, had joined me for lunch. He was very outspoken in our discussions and had a lot to say on every subject. "I have an undergraduate degree in computers and engineering," he said, "and I play around with these things for fun."

I was quite certain he did; he had an Apple II computer in his apartment, and he said he used it often. As he talked, he drew a simple tree to help me catch on. It looked like this:

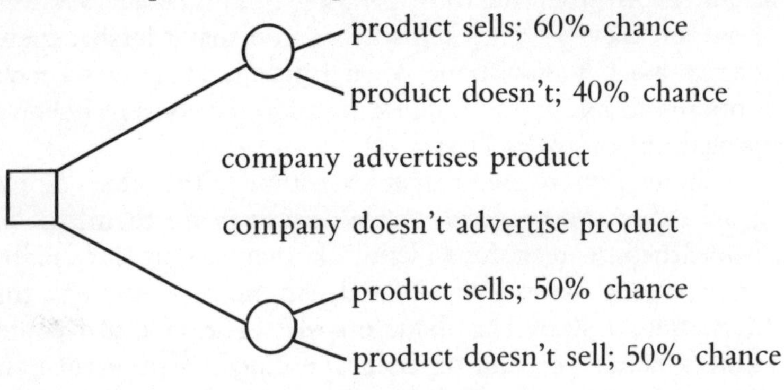

George explained that the decision fork, the box, is where

the company chooses whether or not to advertise. The event fork, the circle, is unknown, but managers can estimate how much advertising improves the likelihood of the product selling. The tree has value when the amount of profit expected can be multiplied by the chance of success. He started to put numbers to the tree, but I stopped him because my head was spinning.

He was friendly and helpful, but as we got up to go to class, I realized how hard it was for him to understand my position. He knew decision trees the way he knew basic math, and it was hard for him to grasp the fact that to some of us it was a new language.

By the time I got to class, I felt a full-blown case of math anxiety coming on. I was neurotic about tackling this subject because it seemed as if I was the only person who couldn't understand anything about ME. Our professor did little to relieve my agony. He introduced himself as Joe Horst, and while he had an impressive string of credentials in decision science, he was, like my Marketing and Control professors, younger than I. Did he have enough experience to teach me economics?

Joe jumped right into the case and in no time we had a decision tree on the board. He explained the usefulness of the event fork and told us that we would work on assessing probabilities. I knew it related to business decisions and I was sure the tree was a useful tool, just the kind of thing I had come to school to learn. But to distinguish act forks from event forks and understand what costs were attributed to what branches of the tree was impossible.

As the class day ended, I felt worn out from my efforts to learn new jargon in Marketing, Control, and Managerial Economics. I could deal with Organizational Behavior because the course drew on what I knew from my training in psychology, but these other three stretched me past my capacity. To relieve some of the tension I decided to run and headed toward the campus track. Once there I was pleasantly surprised to find Kate and we paced ourselves so we could run and talk.

"How are you doing, champ?" I asked. "I thought you did very well today in Marketing. How do you feel?"

Kate looked at me with a sensational grin. Her face shone with her accomplishment. "I can't really judge how I did," she said, "and it almost doesn't matter. All I know is that I won't be called on to open Marketing again, and I am blessed to have it behind me."

"Is that the way it works? I'm amazed. But on second thought it is sensible—because there are fifty-three classes and eighty-seven students in Section D. Even if Rhinehart calls on a different person every day, thirty-four of us won't have to open."

Kate laughed. "Yeah, maybe we could do a decision tree on the probabilities of being called on. Did you understand that stuff in ME?"

"Are you kidding?" I said. "I've got a full-blown, rampaging case of math anxiety—worse than I ever had it before coming here. See? I'm sweating thinking about it."

I yelled toward the sky in a totally useless gesture, "ME makes me sweat more than running an eight-minute mile!"

We ran in silence for a few minutes. Then Kate said, "Maybe you should consider a study group. I started mine last night. There are five of us and we get together in the morning and at lunch to talk over the cases and give one another support."

It sounded like a good idea, and I thought about it later as I started in on the next day's work. Pat also said it was a good idea; she had already investigated the possibilities for herself.

She talked to a few people who spoke in class the first day and said there were four who were interested. All of them wanted to meet at 7:30 each morning and spend fifteen minutes reviewing each case. I recognized the names: Alan Talmadge, the Harvard man who started OB on the first day; Michael Mitchell, whom I knew from Kresge dinner conversations; George Cohen, the computer person who had helped me with my tree; and Sarah Ann Collins, whom I'd spoken with only briefly. Pat invited me to the group's first meeting the next morning.

The more I thought about it, the better it sounded. I needed support, and as Pat described it, it made sense to combine my thinking with students who had different skills. I knew I couldn't do the work alone, but I wondered whether I could contribute anything to a study group, because I only understood Organizational Behavior. I resolved to get up an hour earlier and give it a try.

It was Thursday night and I was grateful for the weekend one day away. I was winding down, needing rest, and decided to go to bed early that night. First I had to go to the campus auditorium to see a required film for Control and then I would get into my cases after a quick dinner. The film was a forty-five-minute explanation of financial statements and was supposed to help us build a foundation in accounting. Tomorrow I had ME, Control, and Marketing classes, and I decided to tackle ME right after the film and dinner.

It was then that I thought briefly about Production and Operations Management and Management Communications. I wouldn't have these courses until next week and I was curious about what they'd be like. Production and Operation Management was supposed to give us the ability to manage technology in the production process. We were expected to learn process analysis; tradeoff analysis; operating systems; capacity management; technological change; and how to develop a manufacturing strategy. I'd heard that our professor, Duke Moore, was a heavyweight among the faculty. He was widely regarded as one of the best professors at the school, and it was rumored that *Fortune* magazine would soon list him as one of the students' favorite business school professors in the country.

The Management Communications course would start Monday. Its purpose was to teach writing and speaking skills, and our professor was a woman, Margaret Price. I looked forward to our class with Margaret because the first few days of class were so heavily male dominated. We only saw women when they waited on us in the school cafeteria, cleaned our rooms, or gave us the day's cases at Baker 20. There wasn't any sexism in the classrooms yet—in fact, professors went out of their way to say "he and she" instead of the typical "he"—but it would be a welcome change to see a woman in authority.

Once finished with dinner, I sat down to do the Managerial Economics assignment, which required me to read about decision analysis and complete a product scheduling decision for an engineering company. I read the assigned chapter in *Quantitative Methods in Management*. It touched on some of the concepts we had covered in class, but the text explanation was much more dense and full of new terms, like *risk aversion* and *expected monetary value*. Then I turned to the engineering case, but it wasn't in my book. This can't be, I thought. When I looked further, I discovered the pages in my textbook were missing. The thought occurred to me that this might have been planned to frustrate me, but I dismissed it as a paranoid reaction. Pat was in the library because she found her room too small to study in, and I couldn't ask to see her book.

I was too tired and annoyed to ask anyone else, so I opened the Control case, about a company called Chemalite. We were asked to draw up T accounts for the company's business. T accounts are the way accountants keep track of a company's money. I drew a dozen *T*'s on the page and labeled them: cash, inventory, and whatever else was on the balance sheet. Then I stopped, since I hadn't any idea what else to do. I decided to call Joyce Freeland, my business partner, and ask for advice.

Joyce Freeland and I had formed a partnership before I had come to Harvard. She was a CPA and she had many years of experience working with business problems. My skills in general management were already useful to clients, and my education at Harvard would bring me up to date with the latest successful business methods. We'd known each other for years and had become close friends, which made our business partnership a pleasure to work in. I needed her advice badly right now and called up to ask whether she could help me with T accounts.

"What's going on? Your voice sounds strained," she said.

"Well, I just have to get these T accounts down. If I understood them, maybe I'd know how to do income statements and balance sheets."

Joyce sounded miffed. "I haven't talked to you for days; it might be nice if you asked how our business was doing or told me how school was going."

"I wish I had time, Joyce, but it's already seven-thirty and I have to finish these cases so I can get some sleep so I can go to study group tomorrow."

I found myself talking for over an hour, and once or twice I was close to tears. I got my questions answered when Joyce explained how accountants keep journals of T accounts and transfer balances to financial statements once a month or so.

When I hung up the phone, I felt comfort at having shared my fears, but I immediately panicked when I realized what time it was and what I still had to do. After hours of more work, I got to bed at 1:30 and when the alarm rang the next morning it was still hazy and dark.

Pat and I met with the study group at 7:30. Everyone was there on time even though one or two came from off campus. I looked around at my group. Michael Mitchell was now a familiar face, for I saw him at meals and his dorm residence was on the same hall as mine. He sat only a few seats away in class and I had ample time to study him. He was a very friendly man, about twenty-eight, and full of unplaced energy, as though he were never comfortable doing exactly what he was doing at the moment. I could imagine him becoming a friend, but I wasn't sure if I wanted to encourage that. He had a way of changing moods quickly; he could be soft one minute and crack a whip over your head the next.

George Cohen was the stereotype of the bright Harvard student. He seemed to know almost everything we studied, and whatever he didn't know he learned with ease. He had a hard time listening, though, and I didn't say much to him. Alan Talmadge was a wonderful person, in terms of his personality and his style. Perhaps I saw him that way because he and I were in the same predicament—we didn't understand much about Control or ME—and because his interest in the arts made me curious about his life plans and his future. When Alan asked me how I was doing, I knew he meant it and I responded by sharing my fears about the numbers courses with him.

I looked forward to seeing Pat Worth in the study group setting. She was very bright, but at night we studied alone most of the time and I didn't have a chance to hear what she had to say about our cases. I was beginning to discover that Pat was, in spite of her intelligence, just as insecure as those of us without quantitative backgrounds. The insecurity seemed to be generated by not knowing whether she had done her work right—which none of us knew, because class always ended with what seemed like hundreds of solutions on the board.

Sarah Ann Collins was the only person I didn't know at all. She looked rested and comfortable in her role as a student and I wondered how she managed to do it. Sarah Ann was about my height, five foot five, and she had wavy auburn hair. When she spoke, she had the sweetest sounding southern speech, a tone northerners don't hear often. I remembered that she had a background in computer science, and her ease with the program began to make sense.

We sat on the edge of our seats and pulled out papers and began to review each case. I'd done my best on each one, but when George Cohen showed us his tree for the ME engineering case, I sat back, feeling like I hadn't done any work at all. I'd missed two event forks completely. When we went over the Chemalite case for Control, I was dumbfounded to hear Pat and George talk about income statements. They ticked through each line on the statement as though it were second nature. We had to rush through our Marketing case because we'd spent too much time on the others and we were almost late for class.

As we rushed to our seats and settled into them, Kirk Cranston called the class to order and said, "Fran Henry, if you were the owner of Chemalite Company, what would you do with the information presented in the case?"

I started to turn red as I sat up stiffly against my seat. Was I called on to open? He had to be kidding. There are eighty-six other students in the class, Kirk; why not call on them? How could you call on me to open when I have no background in accounting and when I obviously need time to get used to being in school again? My heart pounded hard; did it show through my shirt? A dozen more questions went through my head before I realized I had to speak, but it couldn't have been too long because Kirk stood in front of me gazing pleasantly, waiting for me to answer.

"Well, I'd keep a journal of accounting entries and be able to show the movement of money in and out of my accounts," I finally said.

I started to recall what Joyce had told me the night before and I said anything that came to mind.

Kirk must have been satisfied. After asking a few questions, he turned to the students who had their hands raised. For the remainder of the class I sat with my eyes wide open. I felt as if I owned the discussion because I had opened the case, and I listened to all the students' responses as though they were talking to me.

I was elated and relieved and worried all at the same time. I had no idea of how Kirk viewed my responses, but at least I'd been prepared to say something. At least I had talked, and now, like Kate, I could plan on never opening another Control case.

After class I felt even better. Sheryl Shaw, a woman from the other side of the room, came over and asked me if I was an accountant. She said it sounded like I knew what I was talking about. I couldn't believe it; she was a chemist and she didn't know about accounting either. It was my first realization that there were other smart people in Section D who didn't know much more than I did about some subjects.

The rest of Friday whizzed by, and with Marketing and ME over, I was through with my first week at school. Only one thing bothered me; I was uneasy about grades.

Grades were very important, apparently, because some people were asked to leave the school if they didn't perform well enough. I didn't understand the process of grading at first. There was no mention of it in the admissions material I had received or during my interview when I visited the school the previous year. It seemed to work like this. Each section was graded independently of the others. That meant that I competed to get good grades with only my colleagues in Section D. Each of our ten courses was graded on a curve, and the instructor gave five to ten percent of the students Low Passes and ten to fifteen percent of them Excellents. The remainder got Satisfactories. Even if every single student in the class did *well* by objective standards, five to ten percent had to get a Low Pass.

In first year, we started out with six courses, and four were added after January. Of the courses I took now, Marketing, Control, Organizational Behavior, Production and Operations Management, and Managerial Economics were each worth two credits; Management Communications was worth one credit. If a student got eight credits' worth of Low Passes, he or she faced review and probable dismissal by the Academic Standards Committee.

Ending the Marketing class earlier that day, Thomas Rhinehart had described the grading process. "The faculty believes in the forced curve at Harvard Business School," he said. "The grading process places ten to fifteen percent of this class in the position of receiving an Excellent. Five to ten percent of the class will get a Low Pass. The rest of you will get Satisfactory as a grade. The grade is based fifty percent on class participation and fifty percent on exams, with your midterm grade worth twenty percent and the final thirty percent. The best strategy for a good grade is to speak frequently during our discussions. I grade each class when it's over. If you say something irrelevant it will count against you. Quality of contribution is as important as quantity."

Other professors had described the same process. Bob Murphy, our professor of Organizational Behavior, detailed the grading procedure for the entire year. He said that students with four Low Pass grades would be subject to academic review and probably be asked to leave the school. It finally occurred to me, when I put Thomas's and Bob's statements together, that some people would fail.

Why wouldn't I be the one to fail, I wondered. How can I contribute quality comments when I don't know anything about any of the subjects we discuss? George Cohen and Pat Worth and many others seem to know what they are doing, and with CPAs, engineers, and financial analysts in Section D, who will flunk out besides me?

I thought about it during my evening run and again on the way to dinner with Kate and Todd, who had flown in from Atlanta for the weekend. I couldn't help but bring it up with Kate even though I wanted to meet and listen to Todd and get away from business school conversation. She said that people in her study group had come to the same conclusion. Indeed, three or four students in each section didn't make it through the program. They were forced out by the grading system. Four Low Passes, or loops, as they were commonly known, meant you were out.

I felt a little crazy walking back to the dorm. How had I come to this school without knowing that there was a forced curve and that people flunked out? Even though I was tired when I got back to my room, I found myself reading my admissions material for any indication that Low Passes were important. There was no information anywhere. On registration day I'd read the *Academic Standards Bulletin,* and I reread it as I sat there well past midnight. Indeed, it spelled out the entire procedure.

A gnawing started in my stomach, along with a lot of questions I couldn't answer. My best efforts had always been good enough. Would they be good enough for Harvard? I had always displayed self-confidence in my actions; could I be self-confident at Harvard? My first week was over, but I dreaded the future because it could get much worse.

2

DIGGING IN

I never knew how to play football, but I'm learning fast. The basic point of the game, as far as I can tell, is to make your way to the end zone. Harvard is trying to teach us how to keep our eyes focused on our goal, and by early October the goal has become how to stay at Harvard.

My study group meets religiously at 7:30 each morning, and we don't spend much time chatting. By now there are eight of us and everyone wants to get the work done. Michael Mitchell has taken a leadership role in the group, and he suggested that we each take cases to prepare at night, photocopy our analysis, and present it to the group each morning. Since there are fifteen cases each week and eight of us, we each take two cases a week and provide "backup" analysis for two more.

I like the members of the group and I'm often dazzled by their abilities. George Cohen talks frequently in class and his comments are usually right on the mark, as far as I can tell and judging from the professor's reactions. Alan Talmadge has become a friend. Whenever I talk he gives me an encouraging smile, and he surprises me, because even with his Harvard degree there is no elitism in his manner, he is generous with his time and he shares his feelings freely with me and the group. I especially like Sarah Ann Collins, who didn't say much in the first few weeks but recently has emerged in class and study group with a rare combination of sensitivity and analytical thinking.

Sarah Ann also has a sense of humor, which I discovered when Kate and I were leaving class last week. We had just finished a Marketing case about computer printers and Sarah Ann contributed an important part of the analysis.

Coming up behind us, she said, "Talking in class is so shocking. It's just like taking off all your clothes with someone you like and then remembering that you feel fat."

We laughed and the three of us stood under the portico outside Aldrich for twenty minutes or more, talking about the section. I could easily see why I enjoyed Kate McRae so much. We were very much alike with our humanist training and we were very concerned about women's issues. On the other hand, Sarah Ann would never describe herself as a supporter of women's equality. She lived it, though, and had come to Harvard with an assertive sense of her abilities and her potential. It was her genuine concern for others and her openmindedness that attracted both Kate and me to her.

"If you need any help in ME, please let me know," Sarah Ann said.

Kate and I grinned simultaneously and said, "It's hopeless."

I went on to say, "Every day we learn a brand new technique and must apply it immediately. I try to use what I learned that day, but since we're supposed to be learning something else for the next case, I'm always behind."

"Thanks, Sarah Ann, but I don't even know what questions to ask," Kate said.

Kate left for her off-campus apartment and Sarah Ann and I walked to our dorm. We talked about study group and what it meant to us. It was hard for me to express my feelings, which was a strange feeling in itself.

"I wish I could describe it better," I said. "I'm nervous about going to study group. Presenting my analysis is useful, I suppose, but there's so much pressure to put my thoughts in a form that's helpful to everyone. I don't contribute enough."

Sarah Ann looked at me quizzically. "Well, of course you contribute a lot, a lot more than I do. You understand Organizational Behavior, which I don't, and you have a very good grasp on Marketing."

I went on, "Maybe it's more than insecurity—I need more support than the group can give. We're always so rushed. I need much more time to ask my questions and get them answered."

But my unease stayed with me after we parted. Our conversation reminded me of an incident the previous evening in the computer room. Our Managerial Economics assignment directed us to enter some information on probabilities in the computer and bring the computer's output to class. My study group had decided to do the exercise together, and I was looking forward to it because I knew very little about computers and that was one of the things I hoped to learn from the two-year program. When we met, however, everyone seemed anxious to be finished with the exercise and the person who knew best how to run the computer sat down to plug in the data. There was no room for learning; our efforts were expedient and meant to get us on to the next task as soon as possible.

Our problem was that there were so many tasks. All of us seemed to be in our own universe, struggling to keep on top of the material. And when we reached out to others it was to get answers to our own questions, not to help someone else who looked like he or she might need it. My self-absorption frightened me because I was losing a part of me I treasured, that part which would gladly help other people get their jobs done. Would my education rob me of what made me a good manager? As I dug into my work for the night, I knew I had to do something soon about my mixed feelings.

The next day in class I found myself crouching in my seat like a wounded animal, trapped and without much hope for survival. The work load was getting me down. I tried to pull myself out of it, but everything I did made it worse.

The case method was the culprit. I'd heard about it long before I had come to school. This famous technique was the most unifying element of the Harvard Business School. Articles in journals and newspapers praised it or criticized it, but no one denied that the case method had had an enormous impact on the way business leaders were taught in the United States since the school was founded in 1908. Whole programs at other universities modeled themselves after it. And here I was in the middle of it, drowning in its wake.

The case method requires some explanation. It isn't just the cases that are important to the method's success as an educational way of life, it's the way they are taught. Each faculty member has an agenda with each case that is presented. His agenda includes communicating one or two key concepts, which are drawn out in the class discussion and which sink in to students' psyches after they've had a chance to think about them for a while. Some say that a concept like push vs. pull in Marketing would be better taught by an instructor who lectured about it, giving examples and a summary at the close of class. But educators at Harvard believe otherwise, and the case method provides the vehicle. Our professors aren't expected to be teachers in any traditional sense, therefore, and instead they become adept at being guidance counselors, drawing out from students' comments the things they want to hear, the concepts they want communicated.

From a perspective somewhere above Baker Library it all makes sense. But six weeks into the program I was deluged with the concepts we were supposed to be learning. I decided to make a chart to show what my progress was. I jotted down the concepts we were expected to learn, gleaned from the professors' remarks at the end of the class. I starred each one I didn't understand yet.

Under Control I had: balance sheets; income statements; statements of sources and uses; T accounts; variable costs; accumulated depreciation; lease capitalization; statements of changes in financial position; cost accounting; variances. For Marketing I listed: breakeven analysis; push vs. pull; user vs. non-user; the consumer; product policy; market share; advertising to sales ratio.

For Production and Operations Management there were: process analysis; capacity utilization; learning curve; cycle time; job shop; continuous flow; critical path method. For Managerial Economics: risk analysis; expected monetary value; discounted cash flow; hurdle rate; net present value; time value of money; preference analysis; and continuous probability assessments. I stopped at this point and didn't list anything for Organizational Behavior or Management Communications because I was comfortable with everything that was expected of me in those courses.

By the time I finished the list I was wrung dry. Nearly every item was starred. That meant I hardly understood anything I was supposed to learn, and we were expected to master new techniques every night. How could I expect myself to know a page full of concepts that I'd never heard of before the first of September?

Did Kate feel the way I did, or Sarah Ann? I bet that George Cohen didn't. He seemed to take HBS in stride, one step at a time. To get my mind off the list I called my partner,

Joyce. I started to talk about one of our clients, but tears and anger came to the surface as I told her about how unfair it was to be expected to learn all the things that were demanded of us.

"Remember what you said when you left for school, Fran," she said. "The only person you have to please is yourself. You are the judge of how well you're doing."

Her words did echo my sentiments last summer, but that was dozens of cases ago. I felt stupid for not understanding everything and that was that. Joyce suggested I swim or run and call later, and after I had gotten on my running clothes and sped around the track, I had to admit I felt better.

I showered in the dorm bathroom and took a good look at the urinals on the wall and the plaster chips falling from the steamy ceiling into my shower water. Things looked bad, but they didn't have to be that way. I was determined to change for the better.

I realized I cared too much about my physical environment to live in Chase Hall and decided to look into an apartment instead of a dorm room. I'd work hard, but I wouldn't lose myself in the process and I would laugh and joke around. I'd think about whether I wanted to be in study group or not, whether it was hurting me, by draining my self-confidence, rather than helping me.

When I went to class the next day I felt different. It was Tuesday, October 7, and there wasn't anything special about the day, so it took me some time to figure out why.

The answer came right after I spoke in Managerial Economics. Joe Horst was looking for a list of the options that an entrepreneur had in pursuing a risky venture. Whatever he was looking for, I didn't give the right answer. I sat back in my seat, pleased with myself anyway. At least I had talked. Now I wouldn't have to talk in that class for the rest of the week.

It suddenly struck me that all I could do at Harvard was

my best. I wasn't capable of any more. Nor was anyone else. For the first weeks I hadn't been able to rest or relax without thinking about class. I hadn't been able to sleep without dreaming about the discussions. I had been very hard on myself every night for not understanding whatever concept we were supposed to learn in each case. But it wasn't necessary. The school didn't expect it; I did, by asking the impossible of myself. Perhaps that was one of the things that HBS was trying to teach us—to reach high for impossible goals. But the toll was tremendous. From now on I would do the best I could and it would have to be good enough.

My new attitude changed me, at least for the next few days. I felt much more relaxed when I sat in class and did cases at night. I began to think of other activities to join. There were dozens of clubs, social and career oriented. I decided to be the Section D representative for the Small Business Club and the section photographer for the annual report. I also joined the Women's Student Association, a campus-wide group that focused on helping women students through first year and held career orientation sessions for second-year women.

Each section in first year elected WSA representatives, and the women were also encouraged to meet as a group within their sections to provide some support for each other. Danielle Murray and Devaki Gupta were elected as section reps, and they quickly organized the dozen women of Section D who had joined WSA to meet every other week for lunch.

Devaki Gupta had an interesting background, and I was pleased she was a rep for us because I wanted to get to know her better. She was trained as a CPA in India and was planning to return there with her husband, who was also getting his MBA from a university in the Midwest. They commuted on long weekends and both looked forward to going back to India when Devaki graduated in 1982.

Danielle Murray was a woman I took an interest in, too. She was from Nebraska and had never been east before. In all her twenty-four years, she said she'd never seen as much garbage and traffic as there was on Cambridge streets. But Danielle was a street fighter, and when she got into an exchange with someone in class, she didn't let go until the professor called a truce. She was the only woman among us who took an active interest in intramural sports with the men, and she played football, soccer, baseball, or volleyball nearly every day after class.

I looked forward to our first WSA meeting and the opportunity to talk with the women of Section D whom I didn't know yet. At our first meeting Kate was there, as were Sarah Ann, Susan Mantero, Carol Mathias, Sheryl Shaw, Danielle, Devaki, and I. I wondered why other Section D women didn't join, and when I asked Danielle, she said it was because they didn't want to be associated with a women's group. Apparently they feared a feminist label and preferred instead to struggle through the program without the support of other women. I was happy to be part of the WSA, though, because it was fun and helpful to sit around and talk about our fears without anyone else listening.

We shared what we'd heard about other sections and what we'd learned from our visits with professors. Since visiting professors was a formality and we had to make appointments to see them rather than just drop by, news of what they said and what they were like was always highly topical. I was relieved to learn that none of us had any bad experiences yet with our professors.

Because I had worked in the women's movement and was interested in equal opportunity for women, I asked my WSA companions whether they'd ever experienced discrimination and found it very curious that few could say they had.

I wondered why. There was a lot of competition to get into Harvard Business School. Perhaps these bright women, with their finely honed skills, had no reason to fear discrimination. But the more we talked, the more I realized that a lot of the discrimination they would face was ahead of them. Most still believed that you were promoted on merit alone; they'd have to live more to experience some of the subtle and not so subtle ways they could be held back.

Then, too, a feminist awareness is sometimes slow in coming, and sometimes it doesn't have to be labeled as such. One day at lunch in mid-October we discussed Mary Cunningham, who was a vice-president for strategic planning at Bendix Corporation and a top honors Harvard MBA of 1979. That week her name had been plastered across the pages of the big newspapers because the board of directors at Bendix was upset over her rapid ascent in the company. She and the president of the company, William Agee, were alleged to have too cozy a relationship, as they had been seen traveling and entertaining together. But what really bugged Kate was the way William Agee handled the matter and how it was seen in the papers.

"Despite her competence," Kate said, "she is seen as a bad person. Agee called a meeting of the employees to announce that nothing was going on. Now that sounds ridiculous."

"Why is it that we always end up on the wrong side of the moral question?" I asked.

This story reminded Danielle of a conversation she had had with a woman from another section. In the middle of talking, they were interrupted by a man who told Danielle's friend that she was getting quite a reputation on campus. It seems that in squash she beat every man she played; their egos were bruised and suffering. Danielle said that her friend visibly cringed and she couldn't feel proud and happy about her accomplishment. She'd insulted them by beating them.

Danielle went on to say, "And that reminds me of a conversation I had on the way from class to lunch. Stan Hooper, from our section, came over and said, 'Smile, Danielle, you make me happy when you smile.'

"Smile? Why should I smile for you? I'm just as exhausted as you are. I don't feel like smiling and I'm not here to entertain you or anybody else.

"'Wow, that WSA stuff must be something,' Stan said."

Danielle laughed when she told us. "I guess I was a little hard on him. But damn, it's tough to be in this male-oriented culture and not feel some anger."

We were about ready to break up and head back to class when Susan Mantero spoke up. We all stopped to listen; she didn't speak very often and we were eager to hear what she had to say. Susan was from the Southwest, a Hispanic woman with gentle eyes and a master's degree in mathematics. Susan said she might need our support because she didn't know what to do. She was having trouble in one of her courses and had asked someone in her dorm to help her out. He was from another section and he'd said he'd help if she'd go out on Friday night and "have a little fun with him."

Each one of us felt like strangling the guy as we all screamed at the same time, "That bastard. Forget it."

"I'll help you, Susan," Sarah Ann said.

We must have looked fierce as we walked into class that afternoon because even Thomas Rhinehart looked up when ten angry women filed into his class. L'eggs Pantyhose was the case we were to discuss that day, and when Thomas called on Sheryl Shaw to open, there was an audible hiss as the women expressed displeasure at the case, the subject matter, the school, and society in general. We had quite a little support group going in WSA.

One week later I was still trying to do my best, but again I was losing any sense of what my best was. That day we did Lowell Steel in Production and Operations Management.

The night before, when I started to work on it, I recalled the kind words of a close friend, now an advertising executive in New York City. Holly Winthrop had graduated from HBS in 1978 and she was always ready with helpful advice.

"When you get to Lowell Steel, call me," Holly had said. "Remember, they want you to feel the way you do. They break you down to little pieces and then, around February, start to build you back up."

When Holly had given me that advice the previous summer, I hadn't really heard it. I had thought of myself as an emotionally stable and strong person. I couldn't imagine an educational experience breaking me into little pieces. But when I started to work on Lowell Steel, I recalled her advice and found myself dialing her number.

"Holly, this is bad, really bad," I said. "I feel dumb all of the time."

"Yes, I remember Lowell Steel—all those billets, bars, and rolls of cold pressed steel. You're supposed to work out a diagram to show wasted steel or something, aren't you?"

"I think so, but it's already taken two hours to try and understand the steel milling process, so I have little hope of figuring out the specifics of the case."

"Don't worry. I bet the rest of the class is suffering too," Holly said.

Once I thought about it, I knew she was right. Class was actually getting a little bizarre. Some people had lost weight the first weeks of school and some looked ten pounds heavier. One student, who sat a seat away from me, brought candy to every class and munched continuously. I noticed other students developing strange nervous habits. One man pulled on a little fringe of a beard he'd grown since the first day of class; another rubbed a mole on his hand whenever he spoke in class. It was beginning to look red and irritated. One student in the skydeck made me very nervous. Whenever he spoke his voice would change to a high pitch, and he leaned forward in his chair. His hands shook and his voice quavered as he tried to talk. He must have been under incredible pressure because the veins stood out on his neck and along his temples. It was always a relief to see him stop talking and settle back down in his chair.

I had my own stress symptoms which bothered me. For the past three days I had felt searing tooth pain every time I drank coffee or cold water. When I went to the university dentist, he said I had a dead tooth and scheduled me for a root canal, starting on the weekend.

"How can that be?" I asked the dentist. "My teeth were perfectly fine when I went to the dentist last July."

He asked where I was a student, and when I told him, he nodded knowingly.

"Well, stress can kill a tooth, and perhaps this is what happened to you. The MBA program is infamous for stress on students."

Hardly consoled, I walked back to campus. I began to develop a fantasy about writing a letter to Dean McArthur. It would read like this:

"Dear Dean McArthur: It's 10 P.M. Do you know where your students are? Do you care? They're developing nasty physical symptoms. They're smoking dope and snorting coke to relax. Every Friday afternoon most of them drink themselves to oblivion. Do something, fast. Sincerely, Overworked."

My fantasy was corny, but a lot of what I observed was not. There were people in school who snorted coke to relax after getting through cases. And the way we drank alcohol could make anyone nervous. Students seemed to have an obsession with drinking and doing it late into the night seemed to be the way to cope.

There were stories about students on the edge of nervous exhaustion, and two section mates consoled me on my root canal, telling me that they'd just had one each themselves. A twenty-two-year-old student, Melanie Pappas, talked to me about her experience at the Harvard Health Service. She had started to hear a clanging in her ears at night and the doctors couldn't find anything wrong. They'd ordered a full battery of tests, and when she told me about it, tears came to her eyes.

"I think it's just that I'm scared. Scared to fail."

I understood what she meant. Failure seemed just around the corner as we worked hard each night and got overwhelmed each day. By now we were six weeks into the program and we had a section party to celebrate our one hundredth case. Having completed that many, we had only seven hundred to go before graduation. I was glad to go to the party because it was our first social event, and I made it a point to talk to people I'd watched in class but never spoken to. I talked about the pressures of time with Irene Lenkowski, who had given birth to a son shortly before coming to school.

"It's such a rush all the time that I don't see John as much as I'd like," she said. "I get to study group by seven-thirty, and I live twenty-five minutes away, so that means I don't get to see him very long in the morning. Then I get home at five or six; by then I've done a case or so in the library at school. But after cooking dinner for my husband and playing with the baby for a while, I have to get back to my work. It's a tough grind."

I was amazed by the people with children. There were three men and one woman with children under six. The men seemed to have understanding wives who took care of the kids, but it must have been hard even for the men to see their children and spend time with them on a regular basis. Richard Travis, a student with a three-year-old, repeated a conversation he had overheard between his wife and his child. When Marnie Travis asked her son whether he was happy, his reply was: "When Dad's finished with his cases!" I bet that hurt.

There were others I respected too. I wondered in particular about the black women at school and how they managed the program, with the dual expectations of proving themselves for their gender as well as their race. It was harder for me to get to know the black women on campus because most affiliated themselves with the Afro-American Student Union rather than the Women's Student Association. Both organizations were set up to help members cope with the program, and if a student was active in one, she probably didn't need both.

But I wondered whether the black women on campus got the support they needed, and talked about it with Marsha Dunlop, the only black woman in my section. Although we sat next to each other, we hadn't had time until the party to talk about how we were doing. It was clear from our conversation that Marsha was struggling just as hard as I was.

"I came here feeling okay about myself and thought I had worked out a lot of the questions about what I wanted and who I am. I didn't worry about other people's attitudes, just my own.

"But there are so many people here who have never dealt with women or blacks as equals that in order to talk with them about cases I have to spend precious energy educating them first about my competence. And it wears me down. I think that's why I've joined the black students' group—because white women didn't reach out and invite me in, while the men in the Afro-American group did."

I realized as I talked to Marsha that we were lucky to feel supported by the people we reached out to and I wished the same for others. It meant so much to hear other students say, Go ahead, we know you can make it. When I thought about that I recalled Pam Ling, a Section D woman from Malaysia who had never before been out of her country. She'd been a bank manager in Kuala Lampur and left her husband for two years to attend school. How she managed to deal with Harvard Business School was a mystery to me. I wished I had time to get to know her better.

Kate walked up to me and said, "Did you know that two women in our section, Joanne and Melanie, are leaving? They decided yesterday."

I didn't know and it shocked me.

"They reasoned they weren't getting enough out of the program; it just wasn't what they had in mind when they came," Kate said. "And Joanne said she wasn't willing to put up with the changes she saw in herself."

As I headed back to my dorm, I was pursued by the meaning of what Kate had said. I was beginning to see some changes in myself that I didn't like, changes that made me wonder whether I'd become someone else after two years at Harvard. I recalled certain small events happening around me.

Most obviously, there was a growing tension to be first, to get ahead. Even in the Pub, waiting to pay for coffee, people had to move fast, count their change, get through the line. When I didn't move fast enough, someone would invariably cut ahead without so much as a nod. Rude behavior was more acceptable here than anywhere I had ever been, and at times I even found myself joining in. For example, today I had become very angry in class when I heard a student make exactly the point I'd shared with him at lunch an hour before. When I questioned him on it, he said he'd assumed I wouldn't use it since I had already spoken in class. He had stolen my idea, I was mad, and I didn't even know why.

Priorities were shifting and people felt at ease with putting themselves first, before anyone else. I was very uncomfortable with it, with myself.

At the party I had listened to Susan Mantero tell me about

her sick father. He'd developed prostate cancer and called her up to tell her about it. She looked at me and said very sincerely, "He doesn't even know what problems are. I have problems. I'm the one he should worry about." I stared at her, dumbfounded.

Kind people like Susan were getting bent out of shape and starting to talk and act strangely. Even my study group was getting out of hand, and I couldn't do anything to change it. We were trying to help each other in the fifteen minutes we had to review each case, but it didn't feel much like help when one person would interrupt and change a subject that another one of us was pursuing.

A few days ago, during the Lowell Steel case, George had backed up Alan in preparation for the study group discussion. We had heard that Lowell Steel was a tough case, and I respected Alan for wanting to tackle it, because his background was a "no-numbers" one, like mine.

Alan handed out copies of his analysis and started to explain what his approach was. George almost immediately handed his out too, only his was so sophisticated that I couldn't begin to grasp it. I felt hopeless, not having the faintest idea of how to structure Lowell Steel. Alan didn't look very happy either, and I knew he was disappointed with his efforts when he said, "I guess I should have used my calculator to crunch every number in the case."

I gave him a weak smile as we got up to go to class. I laughed a little too, as I did every time I heard the expression *crunch numbers* because it summed up my stereotype of Harvard Business School students. I could easily fantasize about the concept by imagining I was trying to do a case in Production and Operations Management. I'd look over the exhibits carefully with their tables and graphs. Finally, in exasperation, I would tear the numbers off the page and eat them one by one, like a jungle animal eating bushy plants. Crunch,

crunch, crunch. Numbers would get devoured and magically understood.

The everyday conception of crunching numbers was much more mundane than my fantasy, however. Crunching numbers was B School jargon for entering numbers into calculators. It meant getting out my calculator and running through a series of steps to try different kinds of analysis with the case material. My problem with cases like Lowell Steel, and Alan's too, was that we easily lost sight of our goal in doing a case. We'd punch in one set of numbers and then another and then another and forget how to tie it all together. And then it would be late and we'd have to move on to two other cases.

It was rumored that a few students took short cuts to get through their cases. This would be easy to do, because most of the cases we analyzed were used year after year. They were classic examples of a key concept, like breakeven analysis, and professors couldn't resist reassigning them. Using someone else's work, however, was strictly forbidden, because the real value of the case method was in sitting down and confronting unknown material, grappling with it, and coming out with an answer. If a student took a short cut, she or he had wasted time, at least according to the faculty.

It was very damning if a student was caught in class with information not known from the case, and if students found out information not in the material before class, they took pains to disguise it. I had to admit I was impressed with the way the honor system worked; even with the pressure of wanting to do well, I never heard of cribs on cases being sold to struggling students.

School was getting to me, no matter what means I employed to try and control it. The pressure affected even my family life. It was the third week in October and I was pleased for the chance to escape to New York to attend my sister's wedding. I hadn't seen my family since the summer, and I looked forward to visiting with my two brothers, my parents, and of course my sister and her husband-to-be. My sister was thirty, and since she had wanted a small wedding, I was the only female attendant at her ceremony in the United Nations Chapel. She had an elegant reception planned, and though there was little for me to do that day, I walked around in a daze trying to get hold of myself.

School had me all turned around. I could hardly think, much less interact with family and friends. The pain of my sore tooth stayed with me all weekend; it was a hurtful reminder of what I had to go back to on Sunday night. And while everyone looked solicitous as they heard my story, there was nothing they could do to help. I could see a lot of worry in my parents' eyes as they took in my ashen face and thinner frame. They wanted to support me, I knew, but they couldn't accept the way I looked or acted.

"You're not quite yourself," my mother said. "You seem off in a cloud somewhere."

I was off in a cloud, Harvard's cloud. There was an ominous pressure bearing down on me, a pressure to conform and produce. It was slowly forcing me to put other priorities away and put Harvard first. I wasn't really there for my sister that weekend in October of 1980. My mind and body were back on campus, still focused on what I didn't understand about Control or ME.

Once back at school, I began to plan for the next few weeks of classes and November's midterm exams. In order to be prepared for the exams, I had to review the course work in each class. And in order to do that, I needed to visit with each professor and get some feel for how well I was doing. I had no inkling of whether I was an average student or whether my professors thought me stupid or especially bright. There was no planned interaction between student and professor and there was no mentoring system established. Professors rarely gave an indication of what they thought about a student's work in class, so most of us felt insecure.

To start the process of evaluation I began a chart that I labeled "Self-Assessment." On top of the page I wrote each course name and made a column under it. On the left-hand side of the page I listed the weeks of the semester up until midterm exams, which were scheduled for November 17–21. After I drew in the blocks, I numbered each one and then started a list for each number, detailing how I felt about the course that week. I filled in as much as I could remember about the first weeks of school, but the list was beginning to look very top-heavy with things I felt insecure about. I allowed myself a green star for every time I could recall feeling good about myself. There were only two green stars in the first several weeks, even though I had talked at least once a week in most courses. When I finished the list, I decided I needed more information about where I fit in.

Slowly I dialed the professors' numbers and made an appointment to see each one. I wasn't eager to do it, because I honestly didn't know what to say. I couldn't show them my list and tell them I understood nothing, and besides, they probably heard the same thing from half the students in the class.

Thomas Rhinehart was first. I saw him on a Tuesday afternoon in late October, right after Marketing. After the initial pleasantries, he asked why I'd come to see him. I explained that I wanted to know how I was doing and I needed his advice on things I didn't understand.

"Your class is a very emotional experience for me, Thomas," I said.

"Oh, how so?" he asked.

"Well, I felt as though I had a grasp of marketing before coming to Harvard. That is, the concepts we are becoming familiar with make a lot of intuitive sense to me. But the classroom is like an encounter group; everyone seems to throw out anything that comes to mind. And my analysis at night doesn't seem focused."

Thomas looked tolerant. "That's all right. It's the way you're supposed to feel."

I started to tell him of my fears about the class, how hard it was to talk. I told him that he had a lot of power in the class; he should use it wisely, I offered. When he asked me what I meant, I mentioned an incident from that day's discussion.

"I remember the first day of class, when you asked us to be on time. Most of the time we are, but today when Richard, on the skydeck, came in late, you whirled around and marked him late in your book. Then you called on Jack to open, and for the first time someone wasn't prepared."

I went on to say, "You were really hard on him, asking him to come and see you. Why do you have to be so tough with us? You embarrassed him and made us feel like you were some kind of dictator."

"Well," Thomas said, "I appreciate your opinion, and all I can say is that it's damn hard to be up there trying to control all of you."

"You don't have to put any pressure on us, Thomas; we already have a lot."

"I know you have pressure, but without it you all wouldn't work. Who would be crazy enough to work as hard as you all do if you weren't forced into it?"

I left his office shaken. I'd tried to reach out and show him how I felt, but I hadn't gotten anywhere. I'd wanted to hear him say that he recognized my struggle, that it was noble, that it was worthwhile. Instead, he had scheduled fifteen minutes for us to talk; there were two students waiting to see him when I got out, and the short time I did have hadn't told me much. I started to doubt myself a little, thinking that maybe I'd been too honest with him.

My meetings with the other professors were not very much better. The only difference was that I was a little more careful not to show too many of my feelings. With Duke, my Production and Operations Management professor, I tried to find out where I fit in. He told me I contributed on the fringe of the discussions without much substance yet.

"It's hard," I said, "when you've never experienced anything about factories, to analyze production processes and learning curves and all that. Will we ever do anything about non-profits or service businesses?"

Duke looked at me strangely, and he said we'd do a few, as though he'd said it a million times before. He probably thought I was trying to please him with my question because I later found out that Duke's specialty was service-oriented businesses.

He was an excellent professor, the very best teacher I'd ever had. Duke had a way with the class discussion that could make each case come alive; the students' comments kept rolling out one after the other, and his end-of-class summaries always left a clear impression of the purpose of the case. But it was also clear that his standards were set very high and some of us didn't measure up. If we'd work a little bit harder, in his eyes, we might make it.

When I left Duke's office I felt a choking feeling in my throat. I wanted encouragement—I deserved it, I thought—for my nightly grind and daily battles. And he had tried to help me, but he just couldn't take the time to hear what might have taken more than a twenty-minute conversation to say. I wanted to tell him his class meant a lot to me, but it didn't seem to matter, and for some reason I walked out of the building in tears.

I was on automatic pilot now, visiting each professor in turn. Kirk Cranston, my Control professor, was a very nice person. I could tell that from class, and because he sat across from me at his desk with the most congenial smile.

"Well, what can I do for you?" he said.

"I've come with some questions about volume variances, and I'd also like to know how I'm doing."

I really did need to know how I was doing in Kirk Cranston's class. I spoke often, at least it seemed so to me, and although I didn't understand a lot of what went on in class, I worked harder at Control than anything else.

"Let's talk about volume variance first," he said. And then he proceeded to explain and explain again what variances and cost control were all about. After his earnest attempt to satisfy me, I leaned forward in my chair and asked about my class participation. I asked how he thought I'd done many weeks ago when I opened the Chemalite case.

"Actually, I don't recall you opening that case," said Kirk, "and your class participation is not very good. I wish you'd contribute more."

I felt lousy. How could he have forgotten all the times I talked?

"My strategy for talking in all my classes, Kirk, is the same as I use in the outside world. That is, I talk when I have something to say. The rest of the time I'm quiet. I don't have a lot to say when we're in the middle of volume variances or whatever because I don't know anything about them."

Kirk looked mildly amused and I began to resent his grin. After all, he was a Baker Scholar who had graduated the year before with the highest honors the school could offer. He was struggling to understand me and to understand why it was so hard for me to talk in class, but it was hopeless and I knew it. He just couldn't put himself in my shoes and I couldn't help him.

When I got up to leave Kirk said, "Try to talk when we begin the case. Try to get your analysis in there, even if it's wrong."

I went to visit my other professors too. Bob Murphy, my Organizational Behavior professor, was also a very kind person. But I'd had a hard time talking with him, I think, because he seemed to care more about the students who were having difficulties than the ones, like me, who understood OB already. He did tell me he liked what I had to say in class, and after a brief chat I was out of his office and onto the street. I saw Kate and flagged her down.

"What kind of luck are you having with your professors?" I asked. "I'm frustrated."

"I know what you mean. And it's so strange," Kate said. "The HBS faculty was one of the things everyone raved about. Professors were tops and really cared about students. At my undergraduate school we had long, informal meetings with our professors and talked about all kinds of things."

"It's sure not like that here," I said. "I've been very disappointed in meetings with them because there's no place to connect, to feel that I even matter. In fact, it's worse than not connecting. When I told a student in my dorm about my plan to see professors, she cautioned me not to show any of my weaknesses when I met with them. If they knew what I didn't understand they would exploit it by calling on me in class and looking for my weaknesses on an exam. With that advice, how am I supposed to learn when it's so hard to show what I don't know?"

Kate looked thoughtful for a moment and then said, "I think what happens is that they give everything they've got to the classroom. And maybe that's the way it has to be with this Socratic method stuff. The real problem may be that they don't dare get to know us, because then it would be hard to give some of us loops."

Kate was struggling with the same subjects I was. We had back to back appointments to see the Managerial Economics professor, our worst course. I waited for her to get out of Horst's office and we walked out of the building together, commiserating.

"He told me to make sure to explain my assumptions on the exam," I said.

"He told me the same thing," Kate said.

"Let's hope we have some assumptions to explain," I said.

We gave each other a sideways grin and rolled our eyes to the sky in pursuit of hope. The exams were only a few weeks away now and tension had built up to a frenzy. Kate and I made a promise to help each other through school no matter what happened after exams. I reached out for her sunny smile as if it were the proverbial lifeline in a rough sea.

"Kate, have a good weekend with Todd," I said as I headed back to my dorm for a Friday night nap. I really needed rest after another week of coping but not knowing what was going on around me. I needed the weekend to take stock of myself and my situation at school, even though it seemed like I took stock of my situation every few days or so. I planned to talk to Holly Winthrop, who was coming for the weekend and giving a talk at Career Day for the Women's Student Association.

Over lunch, Holly and I talked about business school, the subject that overwhelmed my life. I had a stream of questions she struggled to answer.

"One of the hardest things I face is that I've always done well by my own standards and here I just don't measure up," I said.

"You know, Fran, I felt the same way," Holly said. "But I found that even the brightest students felt insecure about their progress."

I had to agree with her. In Section D it was already clear who sought honors because some students contributed comments often and at just the right moment, when a professor was plying us for a special point. George Cohen, Sheryl Shaw, and Stan Hooper were in this league. But they seemed no more settled about Harvard than I was, because they pushed themselves to understand concepts we weren't expected to know, and even if they talked in every class, they criticized themselves for not talking twice.

Holly brought me back to reality by saying, "Fran, you just have to learn to play their game. It's a male game. It's full of bravado and showing how tough you are. Getting out there and strutting your stuff."

"Playing the game at a learning institution? It bugs me, Holly. I am here to try and learn as much as I can, but why does it have to feel like a two-year hazing? I've already proved I'm capable by getting in, I thought."

Hearing Holly reminded me of what the dean had said to us on the first day of school at our one brief orientation meeting. He had told us we were all capable of getting through, but we needed to play the game. After eight weeks of classes it was clear that the game was to talk even if you hadn't read the case and just wanted to make a point.

"Well, they tell you the training is good for you, will make you a top-notch general manager."

"I think it's crap," I said. "What you need to be a good general manager is both self-confidence and humility. This process is draining me of my sense of myself and making me feel insecure and stupid."

Holly looked at me kindly and I knew she was about to show some pity, which I didn't want.

"Remember what I told you last summer. They tear you down to little pieces and then build you up again. You're just in the middle of the tear-down stage."

"Yes, but it sounds so military. Do you know that HBS is called the West Point of capitalism?" I asked.

"It's almost that," Holly said. "Only it's more like a cross between a marine boot camp and a junior high school. You're in the toughening-up process."

"Holy shit, when I graduate, will I still like poetry and music?" I said.

"I think so," Holly said. "I didn't change that much; I just got a whole lot of street smarts I didn't have before."

"You mean Wall Street smarts, I bet. Because I can't see anything in this process that helps me understand how the real world works."

I carried our conversation around with me for the next two weeks. I remembered her words, but still it was very hard to grasp what was happening around me and to me. I was used to being in control of my life; I no longer was. I tried to take control of it, but the daily process of getting through my schedule was much more powerful than I was. Study group, classes one, two, and three; a speaker in the afternoon; a club meeting; maybe a required film or computer exercise; a swim or a run; a shower; dinner, cases one, two, and three; time for bed. It was my day, day after day, even on what used to be holidays. And I just couldn't bring myself to escape it and cut class because every day brought new concepts to learn, and once covered, we didn't do them in detail again.

It was mid-November and midterm exams were just around the corner now. The class was jittery and people had bags under their eyes, dull hair, and more exaggerated nervous twitches. Even the smartest students seemed scared to face exams.

Kate caught my eye one day after class. "Have you ever been mountain climbing?" she said. "I can't wait for Thanksgiving and the week we get off—it's like working for the top of the mountain. I really need that week off."

"But what a brutal exam schedule we have first," I said.

And truthfully, it frightened me. Classes ended on Monday. We had our exam in Organizational Behavior on Tuesday, Managerial Economics on Wednesday, Control on Thursday, and Marketing on Friday. When I saw the schedule I freaked a little, realizing there was no time to study.

Even my study group members were nervous. We met one day for lunch and each of us took on assignments to prepare for joint study effort. Sarah Ann started our meeting by saying she didn't see why we should settle for a mediocre performance—we could do well on the exams if we applied ourselves. I was so out of place; I couldn't compete and didn't even want to. I wanted support and encouragement and I was further away from them than ever. A few days after our lunch meeting, I decided to leave the group, and it felt like a great weight had lifted off my shoulders when I missed my first early morning meeting. I didn't take the time to talk to each person about it as I would have in any other situation. I didn't even know what to say.

"Well, I'm happy for you," Sarah Ann said when she found out I was leaving. "Someone in Stan Hooper's group told me our group was called the megagroup, whatever that means, because we have so many members who look like they want honors."

"Megagroup? Whoever heard of a word like that? I don't even like the sound of it. I think I'll just slip quietly out and work on my own."

I worked out a schedule to study Marketing, Control, and Managerial Economics. I decided to take the Monday before exams off and study Control; that way I could study all day Sunday and not have to do cases Sunday night. I resolved to finish my studying by Monday night because I wanted to rest and have a good dinner to get ready for my first exam.

Exams had an aura all their own. They were four hours long, and each one was a case similar to our regular cases. Second-year students said the most important preparation was to be relaxed and comfortable.

The Women's Student Association held well-attended sessions in Burden Auditorium before each exam. We all received an outline listing the major concepts we'd covered in our cases. Second-year women who had earned excellent grades the year before gave a talk which reviewed each part of the four- or five-page outline. The WSA presentations were the most impressive student efforts I'd seen since coming to the school. It was the first time I felt someone personally reaching out and trying to help.

I was glad to have the review in hand, since we were allowed to bring books, notes, and cases to the exam. But it was scary, too, to read the compact, single-spaced pages and realize how many things I didn't know. I listed and reviewed and defined, and tried to absorb each concept and to see how they related to one another. For example, I knew we'd be expected to draw up a balance sheet, an income statement, and a funds flow statement for Control and I tried to pull out of my cases what I knew about each one. Finally, on Monday night, I quit studying though there were many things I still didn't get.

Later on that night, I pulled a book from the small collection I had brought from home. Last summer I had planned to have time to read and think about other things while at school and I had brought a few favorite books to Cambridge. I scanned the titles and it was almost as if they were in a foreign language: *American Country* by Emmerling; *Memories, Dreams and Reflections* by Jung; *The Mermaid and the Minotaur* by Dinnerstein. They were dusty from not being touched for two and a half months, and it actually made me shake to pull out Carl Jung's book and crack open the first page. I was afraid to read it, afraid that I'd forgotten how to relate to his words. But like a child soaking up some love and attention, I read and read until I couldn't see straight. I needed to reach down to the center of me, to the fiber in my spine, and pull out whatever I could to get me through these exams. I went to sleep confident that I'd done my best and there was little else I could do.

The exams were grueling and I was right to have been concerned. The first one, OB, was the easy one. On Tuesday morning I filed into the gigantic library reading room, taking my place with other first-year students. It was the first time I had any reason to sit down and work so closely with many first years whom I didn't know, because the way we concentrated our activities in sections gave us little chance to meet other students. I sat across from a friendly young woman who had a pile of papers, food, pencils, and pens all around her. She seemed at ease with her surroundings and gave me a wink as our exams were handed out.

The case was the Textile Corporation of America—a very long and involved story about an ailing company and a young manager who comes in to help out only to find himself in the middle of interpersonal struggles among the top executives. It wasn't a hard case to analyze, because we had learned in class to isolate and describe the "corporate culture" of individual companies and then fit in an "action plan" to the environment which someone found himself or herself in. I was halfway into the exam when I reached out for my calculator and punched a number: Texcorp's profit margin for the past five years.

I heard a gasp across the table and looked up to see that the young woman across from me was white-faced. She looked distraught and stared at me, but there was nothing I could do. We weren't allowed to talk to each other during exams, so I gave her a wan smile and kept writing. A few seconds later she slid down in her seat and a proctor came over and helped her out of the room. A sickening feeling came into my stomach as I wrote out my action plan and wrote and wrote some more.

The old part of me, preschool, would have gotten up, gone over to that troubled woman, helped her out of her seat, and taken her to a lounge to lie down. The part of me that was new, that was determined to get through Harvard Business School, just let her take care of herself while I took care of me. My self-respect was even more eroded when the exam was over and I ran into her in the hall. She said she'd felt a cold coming on but panicked when she didn't know what to write on the exam.

"It was even worse when you grabbed your calculator. I had no idea we were supposed to crunch numbers in an OB exam," she said.

When I got together with Kate, Sarah Ann, and Danielle after the exam, I told them what had happened.

"Hey, don't take it so hard. It's not your responsibility," Danielle said.

It wouldn't have been such a distressing feeling, either, if a similar thing hadn't happened two days later in the Control exam. The exam was ridiculous; we had two lengthy questions on entirely different subjects. One question asked us to analyze the case and figure out all the cost variances in a paper board factory. Variances are differences in actual numbers for unit volume, labor, materials, and overhead from the numbers included in the budgeted plan. We were asked to calculate variances and make a recommendation to the president of the company for cost control.

The other exam question concerned a dry cleaning operation. We were given expenses in the case and were asked to draw up, with appropriate bookkeeping accounts, a balance sheet, income statement, and statement of changes in financial position. Then we were expected to suggest a strategy for expanding the business given the financials we drew up.

I worked like a madwoman through the exam. There was no time to look anything up; I just did the best I knew how. Toward the end, I noticed the student next to me looking at my calculator. He was sweating and flushed, and as I looked up he asked if he could use it. I handed it over, but it was a terrible feeling. I needed my calculator; I didn't want him to slow me down. I could hear every student in the room punching away, as though if the keys were punched hard enough the right answer would pop out on the display.

I was agitated now, and even though I could have worked

longer without it, I asked for my calculator back. It sat there in front of me, and my neighbor finally got up and sat in the front of the room on the floor so that he could plug his own unit into an electrical outlet. Was it my fault his battery went dead?

Of course it wasn't my fault, but I couldn't shake the sleazy feeling I had when I jogged around the track later that day. I wasn't accustomed to taking care of myself at other people's expense. And my concept of being a good general manager didn't include learning how to do that. But that's what I was doing in order to get through the obstacles before me.

At dawn on Friday morning I was up and packing to go to Washington, D.C., for our first break, a week-long Thanksgiving vacation. My vacation would be short because I was coming back on Tuesday to look for an apartment. All I needed to do first was polish off the Marketing midterm and get in a taxi and go. I didn't study too much for Marketing; mostly I tried to review the economics of marketing decisions, like breakeven analysis and gross margin return.

But when I started to read the exam, it was like a roller coaster had started and I knew I'd be nauseous for the whole ride. The case was Cumberland Metal; it was an industrial marketing case about cushion pads for pile drivers. It was a product, a subject, and an industry I knew nothing about.

The question was whether we, as consultants, would advise Mr. Stevens and Mr. Miller to sell curled metal asbestos cushion pads to heavy-construction companies. The case laid out evidence for the new pad; it was much more expensive than the old pads but would save time and might save money in the long run. All of the questions that Thomas had asked in our review session came back, one after another, and I pursued each one until I was confused and upset.

Soon after I started on my second reading of the case, I felt that the pads were a bad deal, the evidence was too flimsy, and the change too risky. I also thought asbestos pads posed too much of an occupational risk to construction workers.

We were an hour and a half into the exam when a proctor came into the room and announced that we should look for pages fifteen and sixteen because some students were missing those pages. Sure enough, I didn't have them and I was furious with myself for not noticing. When I got the new material I could see that it included a new section of the case entitled "Research Evidence." The research showed that asbestos pads substantially increased productivity. I could feel myself losing it, going crazy, as I sat in that cold classroom pulling on my hair. I'd already framed my argument, and my conclusion was not to sell curled metal cushion pads. I had planned to start writing my exam in twenty minutes. I could redo all my calculations and come out with a different conclusion, but it would mean half the time to write my exam. Instead, I wrote a marketing plan based on my no-go strategy.

Later, in the taxi on the way to the airport, I came up for air. I remembered reading my exam in the last few minutes before 1 P.M. I had started it out with the greeting "Messrs. S & M" and in rereading I couldn't bring myself to change the message I was sending to the Marketing faculty. I wasn't used to being flip, but I wasn't used to a lot of things I'd discovered in the process of earning an MBA. I was exhausted, beaten down, afraid and, for that moment and the seven days ahead of me, full of the kind of relief that prisoners must feel when someone opens the door and says, "You're free to go."

Everyone said the toughest part was behind me now and I sure as hell hoped they were right.

3

SINKING

I sat up in bed and pushed feverishly to get my quilt off. I was suffocating and had just awakened from the worst nightmare I'd had in a long time. My room was hot, a strange feeling because it'd been freezing cold before Thanksgiving vacation. Maintenance must have turned the heat on while I was gone. My mouth was dry and my heart beat fast and hard. My head was still moving fast as I recalled the dream.

There was a gorgeous horse. It was a chestnut-colored mare and it had strong-looking muscles and big brown eyes. It trotted on the grassy lawn in front of Aldrich and started to gallop when it came into the open field in front of Baker Library. The horse moved very fast, but all of a sudden a wolf came out of the hedges and ran to the mare, catching up with her, and in one lunge grasped hold of her side, tearing away huge chunks of flesh. The mare stumbled; her intestines were spilling out of her and there was blood all over.

That's me, I thought. I'm the horse and I'm being torn

apart and in a savage way at that. I made myself a cup of tea and sat on my bed gathering my knees up under my chin. My heart slowly stopped its racing. I closed my eyes and breathed in again and again, thinking about my situation.

It was Monday, December 1, the first day back at school after our week-long break. I had needed that time off, but it had gone by so fast that by Monday morning I was just beginning to see straight. Most of my time had been spent searching for an apartment, because I knew I wouldn't make it through the year without my music, without my own space. I had found a very nice place and would move into it during Christmas vacation. I had gone back to my dorm room resigned to tolerate the cramped quarters in which Pat and I lived, the locker room smells in the corridors, and the carbohydrates and sugar we were fed in the Pub and at Kresge. But it wasn't these externals that had bothered me and probably caused my nightmare. What had caused the terror was the class I had had that day in Management Communications and how I felt as a result of it.

MC was a course that nearly everyone laughed at. At first I hadn't paid much attention to it because my energies were forced toward everything I didn't understand. The purpose of MC was to give us writing and speaking skills and I already felt reasonably confident about my abilities in those areas. What did interest me back in September was the realization that my professor, Margaret Price, was the only female of the ten professors I would have my first year. I couldn't help but notice her gender. There were so few women teaching at the school that the administration couldn't possibly have a rational excuse for it. Of the more than eighty tenured faculty only one was a woman, and it was rumored around campus that the school had just denied tenure to two popular and outstanding female associate professors.

My appreciation of Margaret as a female professor was soon tainted, however. It didn't take very long to discover that the Management Communications department, headed by a man, had nearly all female professors and they weren't granted the same status as every other department in the school. In fact, it was inaccurate to call Margaret a professor, because the designation of MC teachers was Associate in Communications. The MC department didn't enjoy being equal members of HBS faculty. To add insult to this injustice, MC was worth only one credit, while nearly all of our other courses were worth two. In some peculiar way, this status seemed to permit everyone, faculty and students alike, the privilege of making fun of MC. Everything we did in the course was the butt of jokes and teasing. The response by the MC department was understandable and in keeping with true business school tradition. They poured the work on.

The first part of the semester we only had to do one paper a week. They weren't long—usually four-pagers in which we analyzed a case. Now, however, in addition to papers, we had group assignments that required out of class time and simultaneously we each were expected to give a prepared speech in class to our colleagues.

On the first day back from vacation we had an MC class. I handed in my paper, a difficult one to write, for it was on the Bristol Myers Corporation. We were asked to take the position of an executive in the company and write a memo on the marketing of Enfamil, an infant formula, in developing countries. The case material outlined the controversy surrounding Enfamil and we were asked to take a position on the issues presented. The major issue was what responsibility Bristol Myers had in selling its infant formula to people who misused the product.

Imagining myself as an executive at Bristol Myers was the

hard part of the assignment. Writing the memo was not, for I had traveled to countries as diverse as Kenya, Honduras, and Indonesia. Ninety-five percent of the people in those countries are poor. In my experience, if they are encouraged by Western advertising and marketing methods to spend what tiny amounts of money they have on Enfamil, they will do so, believing it is in the best interests of their babies. Mothers who buy the formula stretch it out, weakening its nutrient capabilities, and they also mix it with unsterile water. Babies get sick and die from malnutrition and dehydration, and mothers who start on formula and then want to switch to their own milk can't, because theirs has dried up.

In my mind it was a clear issue—infant formula should only be sold in hospitals or orphanages as a life-saving product. Because so many mothers are poor, because there is very little or no clean water and virtually no sewage facilities, infant formula should not be marketed in the broad Third World markets, no matter how big the market or how high-quality the product.

I went to MC class expecting little controversy. It didn't occur to me that people would have much reason to disagree. But in class we had a debate among the four people who were scheduled to speak that day. Two advocated selling the formula—one was Devaki Gupta, co-rep for the Women's Student Association. The other advocate was Stan Hooper, the engineer who was my favorite supporter of free enterprise. The arguments presented to us were nothing new. It was just that I felt like crying when I thought of some of the women I'd seen when I'd traveled. Their eyes had had a longing look to them and I hadn't been able to answer the question about why so many of their babies and even they would die so young when the children I would have could live seventy or more years.

When it came time to ask questions, I saw my roommate's

hand go up and heard her speak about the unfairness of withholding a good product from the market. Pat agreed with Bristol Myers' assessment of the need for infant formula for families who cannot produce their own milk. She reasoned that those (like me, I thought) who wouldn't sell infant formula were "playing God" and the real crime was to take choices away from people. The role of business was to bring good products to market; the rest was up to the consumer.

Michael Mitchell disagreed with Pat, and he raised his hand and said so. He voiced some of the same arguments I had used in my paper. Then Rudolf Ziegler raised his hand. He was a West German economics whiz and he usually spoke only during our "numbers" discussions in ME and Control. He agreed with Michael and thought Bristol Myers' position unconscionable. I sat back and watched the whole discussion like a spectator at a tug-of-war. It was confusing. The people whom I felt most in sync with were a universe away from me in their views. I was settling in for a meditation on where I fit into all of this when Margaret interrupted the discussion. I think it was getting too heated for the teaching purposes she had in mind. With Bristol Myers we were supposed to learn persuasive techniques and argument, but the class was wallowing in rhetoric when she said, "All right, let's discuss a subject we haven't had a chance to get into yet. I asked you to read a chapter in Zinsser's *On Writing Well*. Fran, could you comment on Zinsser's approach to the use of the words *chairman* and *chairperson* and whether or not you object or approve of one or the other."

Gee-zus, Margaret, how could you call on me? In September, you called on me to start the first class and case we had. How could you call on me again? What really bothered me, though, was the fact that I hadn't read Zinsser and had no idea what his opinion was. I was caught unprepared for the first time. It didn't matter if it was the first day back from

Thanksgiving vacation and I had a case to read and paper to write for MC; regression analysis, a new subject, in ME; and a case on emergency ambulance services for POM. What mattered at that moment was that I hadn't read the chapter in Zinsser, and all I could do was stammer out a weak, "I'm sorry, Margaret, I didn't get to it."

I knew it didn't matter that much. But I felt as though I'd let her down, and on a subject about which I had a lot of opinions. When I thought about it, I realized that she had called on me because I had a background in the women's movement. Presumably I would want to talk about the subject. By the time I'd finished with my rationalizations and focused back on the class, I heard Kate answering the same question Margaret had asked me.

"My experience," Kate said, "is that a lot of women want to be called chairman. Frankly, it's not the way I feel. I'm a woman and I love it. I want to be recognized as a woman, not as a woman wearing a man's title. But in Georgia, where I was the staff person for the state arts organization, the 'chairman' was a woman and she was highly insulted if you called her anything but."

Sheryl Shaw raised her hand. I wondered what she would say because I didn't know her feelings about being a woman in the corporate world. She shocked me and made my whole being sit up and listen when she said, "It's not just words like *chairman* and the generic *he*. It's language in general that's the problem. The English language used even in our courses is male oriented and doesn't represent women."

The emotions from our previous discussion must still have been in the air because George Cohen's hand shot up.

When Margaret recognized him, he spoke with some anger. "You women are trying to make everything unisex. It's inappropriate and unnecessary."

The class was nearly over as I raised my hand. Margaret

didn't want to allow another speaker because she had to close the discussion, but I must have looked desperate, for she called on me.

"The issue is not whether 'we women' are trying to make everything unisex. The issue, as far as I've heard it articulated in the women's movement, is that language needs to be broadened to include women.

"For example, in Marketing class we routinely use the terms *penetration* and *thrust*. We want to penetrate the market by cutting price and to sell more product. Or we want to reposition our product with a new marketing thrust. These words are sexual words and they are male. They connote power as though male sex were the only definition of power.

"We need to broaden the definition. We need to use words like *envelop* and *surround* and use them with a sense of strength and resolve. Then we've got a representative situation in which we all can live harmoniously."

Class was over and I heard a rustle and a sputter behind me. It was Stan Hooper. His body was leaning over the desk and his jaw muscles were tensing up.

"Fran, I've got to talk to you," he said.

By the time I got up and turned around, Danielle, Sheryl, and Devaki were also there, wanting to join in the discussion.

"What you're saying is totally wrong, because there's no power in strategies which surround," Stan said.

I knew that Stan's background was military—he'd graduated from West Point.

"We learned in school that the only strong offense is to go right at the enemy, the target—and that's just what we learn to do when we penetrate the market."

I got out my pencil and yellow pad. "Here's the target, Stan. And here I am. You can't tell me that it's not just as important to surround a target as to attack it. Perhaps if you surrounded it there would be fewer lives lost."

Stan took the pencil and drew his offensive position. By the time we got through with our circles and arrows our diagram looked almost pornographic, with thrusts and openings everywhere. Neither of us budged.

But I blinked and Stan said, "Fran, I've been going to military school since junior high. Now I'm twenty-nine. For all those years I've been told how to sit, how to eat, how to hold my head, how to think. In this school I experience the most freedom I've ever had. Now you're telling me that the words I've used all my life are inappropriate. Your philosophy takes what little power and freedom I have away from me."

"Well maybe that's what it's about, Stan, sharing power. Try to imagine yourself in a world where everything and everyone around is called 'she.' 'He' is only used to connote fatherhood, the consumer, or the secretary. Imagine your longing to hear yourself referred to as the lawyer, she; the president, she."

"Well," Stan retorted with a grin, "why not get everyone to use the word *she?* It's not a bad word; it even includes the word *he.* After all, in my time, I've been called much worse things than she!"

I realized he couldn't possibly understand how insulting that was. On the surface it was a joke, but underneath he meant every word of it.

And so I found myself, at 3 A.M. the morning of December 2, huddled in a fetal position on top of my bed, trying to orient myself in a place where very few spoke my language. I was trying to figure out my whole world and its conflicts at that point. I wanted to know why Kate McRae's mother had told her she shouldn't come to Cambridge because Todd needed her in Houston. This even though Todd supported her and Kate's dad had graduated from HBS many years ago and, had he been living, would have been proud of her. I wanted to know why the women seemed so reticent to talk in the numbers courses, as though their analysis was not as good as the men's. And I wanted to understand and then change the habit so many women had of raising their hands and starting out their comments with the phrase "I just wanted to say."

I just wanted to say. In class even I said it, as though I were a little girl and finally someone was taking me seriously after making me wait on the sidelines of a game for innings before letting me play. I just wanted to say.

"I just wanted to say I hate this damn place," I said to no one at all.

But saying it and recognizing the hurt I felt allowed me to cry until my anger and hurt were gone. And then I went to my desk and wrote out a few pages of notes to remind me of why I wanted to get an MBA. I needed some special support and validation that wasn't to be found in my professors or my classmates or the things I was learning.

I reviewed the whys again. Why did I want an MBA? Why from Harvard? I recalled knowing years before that I wanted a useful graduate degree, one which gave me practical tools I didn't already have. I remembered hearing about how MBAs could telescope years of business experience into a few months of learning. I remembered, too, that when I had called the Harvard admissions office for the application I was scared that they would reject my voice over the phone, knowing as they must that I wasn't qualified, that I hadn't taken math since high school.

Then I remembered an event that was a kind of turning point in my decision to apply. It had occurred during a business trip in 1979. I was on a plane, flying from London to Bangkok. I flew First Class as there were no coach seats left by the time I booked my flight. While I liked the comfortable seats in First Class, I was dismayed to find the only other women in the cabin were waiting on the men. I had thought I would have my row to myself on the flight, but just before the door closed a stout, balding man in a dark blue pin-striped suit eased himself into the seat next to me.

After we had been flying for a while, he asked about my T-shirt. It was dark blue with a big sun and it said NO NUKES. I explained that I had bought it at a demonstration in Washington, D.C., a few weeks before. And I went on to say the demonstration was to support solar and other alternative energies so that we wouldn't put ourselves and our children at risk with nuclear power. He looked at me with his head tilting one way and his eyes slanting another. I know he thought I was, at the very least, strange.

"And what about you, where are you going?" I asked.

"I'm flying from London to Dubai," he said. "I'm an executive for an oil firm and I've just come from my annual home holiday."

Dubai is the capital of the United Arab Emirates. It was at least eight hours away, so I decided to talk. We chatted about the oil situation and about living abroad. He asked where I was going and whether I was on vacation.

"No, I'm traveling to Bangkok for my company. It's a firm in Washington, D.C., that supports the efforts of developing countries to use appropriate technologies. That usually means, for poor countries, labor-intensive rather than capital-intensive projects. You know, like building many small village hand pumps with community workers instead of building huge dams which benefit only a few."

Well, no, it was clear that he didn't understand. But we discussed these concepts for a good two hours. Basically, he saw things in a way that was diametrically opposite from mine. After a while he gave me a smug grin and stopped talking. A few hours later he spoke to me again, when we were flying over Turkey, and he asked about our meal, which was outstanding. It was clear that he was no longer interested in my opinion on serious topics.

More to be pleasant, I believe, than anything else, he said, "And what will you do with your career?"

I told him just exactly what was on my mind. In the coming year I planned to apply to Harvard and Stanford business schools and get my MBA.

From that moment on he never stopped talking. He asked me at least a dozen questions about politics, about Carter, about the U.S. dollar, about personnel problems. He and I talked for the rest of the trip, and when he got off at Dubai, I was greatly relieved not to have to bend my neck in that direction anymore. I thought and thought about his reaction. How could an English oil executive who worked in the Mideast value an American MBA so much that it overshadowed his distaste for my point of view?

Back in my dorm room with my thoughts, I was exhausted from the strength of my emotions. But I wasn't finished writing or finished with the subject of why I was at Harvard Business School, struggling to fit in against what seemed like impossible odds. I remembered one aspect of the incident on the airplane that was so important to all of my feelings about being in graduate school. It was the power to influence people, the power to be listened to and taken seriously.

So often, it seemed, women lacked the necessary authority to take control of a situation and be listened to. When I thought about my business, Enterprise Associates, and the work I would do helping people market and finance their ideas, I imagined myself sitting in front of a banker and trying to convince him or her to lend money to my client. When that image came to mind so did an MBA. It was there like a silent partner, helping to shore up my credibility.

Thinking about my expectations made me remember the

summer before starting school. It was one year after talking with the oil company executive, and in the interim I had applied and been accepted to school. I took a vacation that summer in one of my favorite spots, Nantucket. While on the island I found a very nice, affordable home and decided with a few other people to buy it. I had to get the mortgage money from an off-island bank, so on the way home I stopped at a recommended one in New Bedford, Massachusetts.

When I walked into the bank and asked to speak to a loan officer, I could tell the receptionist was hesitant to refer me anywhere. It was hot out and I was dressed in tennis shorts, not exactly appropriate garb when looking for mortgage money. A vice-president was free and he sat me down asking about the house, steering clear of answering my questions about interest rates and terms. In fact he talked for ten minutes about his experiences traveling to Washington, D.C., for bankers' meetings and we were both a little bored when he finally said, "And, young lady, exactly what do you do for a living?"

"Right now I'm self-employed," I answered. "I'm a partner in my own business. This fall, however, I'll be at Harvard Business School getting my MBA."

"Harvard? Harvard Business School? Well, well, well," the banker said, "let me see what we can do here."

With a flourish he catapulted out of his chair and headed to his file cabinet, pulled out the papers I needed to apply, and explained the availability, terms, and time schedule for getting my money. He even described how much he liked going to Nantucket to look at mortgagees' homes and said he hoped I could get the papers back before the end of the summer.

I was embarrassed by his behavior, but that wasn't the end of it. When he had finished his exposition he nodded to his secretary, a woman in her middle years who came dutifully to his desk.

"Mary," he said, "I want you to meet this young lady. She's going off to Harvard Business School this fall. Isn't that wonderful?"

Mary gave me a pleasant smile, no doubt because she was expected to. Then our banker went on to say, "Mary's nephew has applied, but he hasn't heard yet. It's such an important education."

My face was quite red by then and I had started to get up when the banker came around and pulled out my chair, dismissed Mary, and walked me out the door.

"Good luck, Miss Henry, I'm sure you'll do well," he said. "Let me hear from you about those papers."

This memory was etched in my mind because it was so close to home. Right in New England, where I wanted to live—bankers listened to me. When I thought about it I smiled, and the smile brought me back again to my dorm room, where I was feeling tired but more peaceful. I would try to stay at Harvard. I didn't want to be better than anybody else and I knew that earning the degree wouldn't make me better. But it certainly did feel good to be equal and that was worth some pain.

For the rest of the week I did my work in a spirit of resignation, having reevaluated and accepted my goal of earning the degree. It was easier to listen to different points of view in class; it was easier to put in the hours at night. Only one thing intruded on my relative peace and that was the unsettling feeling that the work load wasn't getting any lighter. Now we were deep into accounting terminology in Control, learning about different inventory methods and ways to account for sales and income. In the Managerial Economics and Production and Operations Management classes we were getting new computer concepts aimed at teaching us how to rationalize production and scheduling on the factory floor.

Last September we had been given an assurance by the WSA second-year women that the hardest time would be from September to November. After that the pressure would let up and the professors would be easier on us.

I couldn't see it in action yet; it felt just the same to me. The only obvious difference that first week after Thanksgiving vacation was that we didn't have Marketing anymore. When I looked at my year's schedule, I realized that we were finished with Marketing until the spring. For three weeks, until Christmas vacation, we had POM, Control, OB, ME, and MC. In January we'd begin two new classes in addition to our current ones: Finance; and Business, Government, and the International Economy, called BGIE.

These interim three weeks were an excellent time, the second-year women had said, to shore up our grades in the tough subjects by doing our work carefully and by talking a lot. That advice didn't indicate that things were going to be easier—it seemed like more pressure.

In fact my sense of peace during the first week of December didn't last too long. Two concerns loomed large on my short-term horizon. One was not a big deal—it was the MC speech I was required to give on December 16. The other concern was the biggest of deals: all first years would get their midterm exams and grades in Managerial Economics, Marketing, Organizational Behavior, and Control. This was our first feedback from the professors on how we were doing in relation to our classmates. Having worked so hard all semester, we were all eager to know where we stood.

Before this point in early December, it had seemed we were equals. Even though some of us had more education or perhaps more experience, we treated one another on a par. It was true that some students sought honors, but there was no reason to believe they knew more than the rest of us. Now a curious fascination crept up on us. Every rumor about when we'd get our exams back traveled through the section like lightning.

Midterm grades didn't mean that much, all the professors reminded us. Remember, they said, the registrar doesn't get the grades, and the only grade that counts is your final one. If you don't do well, you have plenty of time to make up for it before the end of the year.

But at that point midterm grades meant everything, and finally on December 9, Rick Cabot, our section's liaison with the faculty, stood up at the end of class to announce the schedule. The next day we would get back Control, the day after that OB, and then ME and Marketing.

I could tell that most of us couldn't wait for the next day to end. We practically shoved our professor out the door at 2:30. And in came Rick carrying a box full of manila envelopes. He designed a procedure so that we all got our exams quickly, but even so we were like packs of dogs yelping around someone with a bone. Even if we tried to be nonchalant there was that hunger in each pair of eyes: how did I measure up?

Kate caught my eye and we winked and wished each other good luck. I took my envelope, which was sealed tight and had my student number across the front: 20220. Well, 20220, I thought, here goes, and I headed back to the safety of my room.

It was cold out, down to fifteen degrees, and I pulled my hood up over my ears even for the short walk from Aldrich to Chase Hall. But inside my warm jacket I could feel the sweat trickle down my back. How had I done in Control? In the subject that was the foundation of Finance, that was the guts of my business work? Soon I'd know, and as soon as I walked through my door, I opened the envelope and pulled out my evaluation sheet.

Low Pass. Low Pass. Low Pass. Oh my God, Low Pass. I flunked. I read Kirk's letter to our section. It went:

"I know many of you are anxious about how well you performed on the midterm examination in Control and how I perceive your contribution in class. I hope this letter relieves some of the anxiety.

"In evaluating your contribution to the class discussion, I have tried to consider attendance, attentiveness and responsiveness to peer comments, apparent preparation, response when called on, frequency of participation, brevity and the relevance of your comments. Recognizing that this involves a highly subjective judgment, I have simply divided the section into three approximately equal groups; I—above average; II—average; and III—below average. I would assess your performance as falling into category III.

"The midterm examination provides both of us with feedback on your progress in mastering the course material. A well-designed midterm also contributes to the learning process by challenging you with some new concepts."

And on and on I read until I came to my exam grade, which was Low Pass too. I still had my coat on and my face was flushed hot. I was dizzy and sick to my stomach and I grabbed the side of the desk as I fumbled to take off my coat and sit down.

I read further. Our exam grades were arranged in a histogram, Kirk's letter said, so that we could see where we fit into the scheme of things. A histogram, I thought, what the hell is a histogram? When I turned the page I saw a bar chart—how frustrating to even have to decipher a bar chart to find out where I fit in.

For a few minutes I couldn't see the page. My eyes were swimming with tears because of my fear that I was doomed to fail. How could Kirk have given me a Low Pass in class participation when I tried so hard, when I did the work so earnestly, when I spoke every few classes? I felt cheated and angry.

When I could collect my thoughts enough to read the histogram and finish his letter, I realized that my grade on the exam put me in the bottom quarter of the class but not at the very bottom. As Kirk explained, only ten percent of us would eventually get a Low Pass, so the twenty-five percent who got Low Pass on the midterm were given that grade simply as a warning.

Warning or not, the letter was ominous. I fingered each page of my exam and looked quickly at the sample Excellent exam to which we were expected to compare our efforts. My hastily scribbled numbers embarrassed me now. I thought I had done a creditable job, but I missed so much.

Later in the evening Kate called to find out how I was.

"I did rotten, champ, how about you?" I answered glumly.

"Well if you mean Low Pass, I'm the friend you should have. I'm in the same boat," she said.

We talked and laughed for a few minutes with the wry humor we used whenever we talked about school and how little we knew and how we felt. And we talked again the next night about our grades in Organizational Behavior. We had gotten OB back that afternoon and our grades were both Satisfactory Plus. Bob Murphy, our OB professor, had given each of us a page of notes about how well we had done on our exams. He told us what our exam strengths and weaknesses were. We tried to feel good about our grades, but we didn't really.

"What did we expect to get in OB?" Kate asked. "If we can't get a Sat in OB, it's absolutely hopeless."

"Yeah, Kate, I agree with you. But still," I said, "we

didn't just get Sat, we got Sat Plus, and we shouldn't be so hard on ourselves."

The next afternoon I had to go off campus after school. When I thought about it, I realized it was December 11 and since Labor Day I hadn't gone anywhere after school except to run or to a required event or lecture. But that afternoon I had to catch a bus in Harvard Square and go to a nearby town to pick up a film I planned to show during my speech in MC next week.

When class was over, I got the envelope with my Managerial Economics exam inside and buried it in my backpack, running across the bridge to the bus stop. As I slowed down to a walk, a young man in a preppy-looking green sweater and blue pants walked by me. As I got closer, about three feet away, he quickly unzipped his pants and pulled out his hardened penis. I looked up at his face in shock, as he must have wanted me to do, for as I walked by he smiled triumphantly.

Stumbling more than walking, I got to the bus stop and on the right bus. I felt so vulnerable, so offended by that guy's behavior. I was angry,too—angry at myself for not stopping, spinning him around, and slapping his face. What strange problem did he have that made him exhibit himself, I asked myself through my clenched teeth.

Not long into the ride I remembered my exam. I pulled it out and looked at the back page. My score was 48; the professor had written: "Please come to see me and we can work out a strategy for the rest of the course." When I looked further I realized the 48 was a pretty bad score. It was right at the bottom ten percent of the class. I looked over my exam—my decision tree still looked good to me. I thought the things I focused on were relevant even though my answers were off base to Joe.

I sank into my seat for the rest of the ride. I was alone and afraid and paranoid. Why had that man exposed himself, and why had I gotten such a bad grade in ME? Was I really that stupid? That I'd done a good job on the case according to my own standards and that I must have learned a lot since September were lost to me. I had no perspective except the one that my grade reflected. When I got to the Newton Highlands Library, my destination, I had further proof of my inadequacy. Even though I'd reserved the film and it was waiting for me, I had a hard time talking to the staff at the office. I stammered and found it difficult to ask my questions. It was as though I were in a fog, without any focus or bearing.

Later, I called Kate to commiserate. We had a lot to commiserate about because we'd both done poorly. But Kate thought there was hope because Joe Horst had written a note on her exam requesting her to come to his office and plan a strategy for the rest of the course.

I wanted to lie to her but I couldn't and said, "Oh, Kate, please don't take this too hard, but that's exactly what he put on my exam."

She was disappointed, I knew, because of the long silence on the phone.

"I'm tired, Fran," she said, "tired of being just like a widget on their factory floor. We're all just alike to them, aren't we?"

I couldn't deny it. The same feeling of dislike and distrust came over me when I felt like just another cog in Harvard's giant wheel.

"The hardest part for me, Kate, is facing him in class. Now he knows how dumb we are. Maybe tomorrow will be better. We get Marketing back and then the week is over."

Friday's classes slipped by fast. We were all ready for the weekend and the Section D holiday party at the Harvard Club in Boston. Only one more week of school and then two weeks off for vacation, but there was more tension in the room than usual because many of us were very worried about our grades in Marketing.

Thomas Rhinehart couldn't communicate what was expected of us and most of us had written our exams not knowing what a good one was. Marketing summed up all the emotions we had about school. The cases we read were tedious, and because we never got assignments, we didn't get direction on how to analyze them until well into class. The way Thomas Rhinehart conducted class was bound to make us jumpy. He sped around the room calling on people in rapid-fire succession and there were few breathing spaces in a discussion when he brought together diverse elements of the case. His brief end-of-class recitation was always a series of questions about marketing choices that we, as managers, would face, but we left class with no answers.

The familiar box of sealed manila envelopes was delivered and I carried my exam back to my room, opening it as I opened the others, with anticipation and fear. The cover sheet was the distribution of grades. My head sank to the floor and then my whole body followed. For my exam grade Thomas had given me, along with twelve other students, a Low Pass. For class participation he had given me a Sat Minus. I couldn't believe it. The tears welled up in my eyes and dropped onto the page, smudging the comments Thomas had written out for me. I read:

"Instinct tells me that you are a better student than the above grades indicate."

"Instinct? Instinct?" I heard my voice get shrill with anger. It's not instinct, Thomas, it's hard facts. You know from the discussions that I know marketing better than this. His comments were so cold and unenthusiastic. I felt as if they had nothing to do with me.

I read on. Thomas had taken the time to make comments on each of our exams, and I read through every point and tried to remember why I had taken the position I had. I remembered that I hadn't liked the curled metal cushion pads for construction because they were made of asbestos and because they weren't thoroughly researched.

The fact that they were asbestos had no bearing on the case apparently, for Thomas didn't comment at all on my distaste for the substance. The basic problem with my exam, he wrote, was the fact that I ignored the savings that construction companies could get by using the pad. The evidence was in the research data—the pages I hadn't gotten until too late. And I had multiplied wrong, coming out with an incorrect productivity savings.

That was it. That was all he had written. I read it through again but I couldn't find what I wanted, what I so despcrately needed. I searched for a small amount of recognition that I was a hard worker, that I knew this stuff, that I was not a dummy. There was nothing to help me out.

Marketing. The subject I thought I knew. The classes I worked so hard to speak in. The cases I labored over, trying to capture the most important points. Even, when I thought about it, the course I felt some pride in because I challenged myself to speak and I did speak at least every few classes. I looked back over my week. It was strewn with my bruised feelings and my crushed self-confidence. I had looped three midterms cold. That meant I would get a warning letter from the administrator's office saying I had better shape up. Even though a healthy third of the class would get warning letters, it still was a depressing, indeed a debilitating, thought.

I wasn't ready to do anything yet. All I could do was sit and think. And that's what I did for a few hours or more right through dinner and through the evening. I was relieved at the informal tradition of not sharing grades. At first I had found it remarkable that, at a school famous for its competitive atmosphere, most people were secretive about where they stood. But now I was grateful for the privacy because I, along with probably two-thirds of Section D, felt inadequate.

For the first time I had to consider seriously whether I should stay. Why should I be a masochist and put myself through this? I recalled my interview in the admissions office before I was accepted into the school in 1980.

"Your experience is the kind we look for," Jane Kelting, the woman who interviewed me, had said. "But we do have a few problems with your credentials. One is your math background, another is your description of your weaknesses."

"Math will be hard for me," I said, "but I'll work extra hard to catch up. Actually I was very good in math in high school. I won an award for my honors score on a statewide exam. But I took a calculus course my first year in college and the professor had a thick German accent. I couldn't understand anything he said and I got a C in the course. My guidance counselor told me that since it was a teacher's college and I planned to teach history, I didn't need math, so I never took another course."

"Well that won't be as difficult for you as the other problem." Jane looked at me kindly and went on, "You say that you're shy and that sometimes it gets in your way. That will be a problem at Harvard because, as you know, class discussion by the students is critical to the learning process."

As I sat there in my dorm room about one year later, I remembered my response exactly because it surprised me at the time.

"Yes, I consider myself shy. And I struggle with it. Struggle to speak up and assert myself. But most people don't see me that way. They think I'm quite an extrovert, going around organizing and speaking. My shyness is a very personal view of myself."

Maybe they were right to question me, I thought, when my consciousness brought me back to earth, to my room again. Maybe I'm not good enough. Everyone around me is so smart, maybe I should just forget it. I thought my best work would be good enough, but maybe it's not.

For that night and for the next day, a thundercloud hung over my head. It weighed down on me like some frightful presence that I couldn't shake off. But I couldn't be depressed for too long because Saturday night was our Section D party and Sunday I had to write my MC speech and study for our POM midterm, scheduled for Friday the nineteenth, the last day before vacation.

Nearly all of my classmates were at the party and we were in decent moods. A lot of us were in the same leaky boat and trying desperately not to sink.

"What the hell, let's have a good time," Kate said.

I did. I asked nearly every man to dance, as bold a move as I'd undertaken in quite a while. But I didn't care. I felt like dancing and why not ask men to dance? My assertiveness was exhilarating and propelled me to ask Kirk Cranston. He is a pretty good dancer, I thought. He even has a nice smile. Why can't I learn cost accounting from him?

Even with the joviality, school lurked in the background. It came out full force when the party broke to sing Christmas carols, ones which were rewritten in B School style. I sang with everything in me and even tucked the words to one song into my purse because I didn't want to forget them. It went like this:

> "Jingle OB"
> (sung to the tune of "Jingle Bells")
>
> See him warming up, a chainsaw to command,
> Looking for a student, dumb enough to raise his hand.

Is your idea good, I mean really, really good?
I mean really, really, really, really, really, really good?
Oh!
Harvard profs, Harvard profs, watch them turn the screws.
When a student starts to speak you know that he will lose. Oh!
Harvard profs, Harvard profs, what skill at dentistry,
What's more thrilling than to be drilling
On poor old Section D?

Rushing through OB, at eleven-thirty at night.
Will he call on me? My heart is filled with fright.
M.E. is a bear, I dread it with a sigh.
The computer completely baffles me, after I say "Hi."
Oh . . . bust my balls, bust my balls, bust them all the way,
Oh what fun it is to work sixteen hours a day.
Bust my balls, bust my balls, kick me in the ass,
Oh what fun it is to be the smartest shit in class.

The next morning I woke with a hangover, a rare event for my rather health-food-oriented life. A hammer was banging away inside my head, but a voice told me to ignore it because I had to write my MC speech. My MC speech team was comprised of three men and me; our topic was the advertising policy of the Kellogg Company. Our team had decided to present a panel discussion with the four of us representing various points of view on the case.

The case presented the issue between the Kellogg Company and the Federal Trade Commission. Should Kellogg be allowed to advertise its sugared cereals during children's TV time? Michael Mitchell was on my team and he took the role of a representative of the advertising business. I would have loved the role of the Kellogg spokesperson just because I'd never been in such a position and I wanted to see whether I could think of anything to say. But because I was so exhausted and feeling very uncreative that first week in December, I had offered to take the FTC position. The FTC argument was easy for me to articulate, though my classmates looked at me strangely when I said so. They couldn't imagine choosing the side of *government* over *business*. Richard Travis took the role of consumer, and John Cassidy was the advocate for the Kellogg Company.

I worked on my speech Sunday morning and then studied Production and Operations Management for Friday's exam. Our team was scheduled to meet and go over our speeches at 4 P.M., which would give us plenty of time to do our cases for Monday. At four I went to the Pub to meet the men and pulled out my speech. Only Richard, the consumer advocate, had his done. Michael and John listened as we went over our presentations.

We worked on the lineup. First we'd show the film, which was made by Action for Children's Television and was pro-consumer. Then Richard would speak, and next Michael, the advertising executive. I'd represent FTC next, and John would close the debate. Then we'd take questions from our classmates. It bothered me a little that John and Michael hadn't done their speeches, but I dismissed it. After all, Michael was on crutches because he had torn a ligament in intramural sports the week before, and he was moving a little slowly.

On Tuesday I got ready for MC class by wearing, instead of my usual jeans and sweater, a nice pair of pants and a silk shirt. My teammates all wore suits. We took this seriously—but we ended up laughing a few minutes into the program because the required film had been borrowed by another MC class and not returned in time to begin our debate and because Richard accidently tripped on the breakfast tray that Michael laid out to demonstrate Kellogg's ideal breakfast. There was orange juice, milk, and cereal all over the floor, and as I stood up to speak, I barely could stop laughing myself.

I did stop laughing, though, when John was a few minutes into his speech. His arguments, one after another, were direct refutations of everything Richard and I had said.

He had listened to us and then written his speech. I was so mad I could hardly breathe. What a foolish thing to do, I thought—to let him know what you were thinking. What else did I expect from this place?

I simmered all afternoon. I must have looked like I needed to talk because when I ran into Sarah Ann before dinner she invited me to take a break for a change and eat off campus.

"Let's go right now. It's a great idea," I said.

"Fran, I've got good news. Jack and I are going to be engaged," Sarah Ann said as we settled into our booths at the restaurant.

Jack Tobin was Sarah Ann's sweetheart. He was a smart man, an engineer, who had moved up to Cambridge to be Sarah Ann's moral support when she had come to school. I was very happy for her, but worried in a way, too. This semester we were all under such pressure—perhaps it wasn't the best time to make big decisions.

"He's the one, and I know it," she continued. "He's the kind of person I've always wanted to be with. We'll marry in June and then work for the summer."

"Well, I'm very happy for you and I know you're a woman who knows what she wants."

Sitting in the restaurant and looking at Sarah Ann gave me a chance to think about the women at school. They were no different from many women I knew in so many ways. And yet there was a quality about them that I couldn't exactly pinpoint. It had something to do with determination. Something to do with goals. They, we, were all very determined young women with a healthy dose of independence. We didn't all know what we wanted, but once we did know, we pursued it with a vengeance.

"Oh, Fran, don't you look pensive," Sarah Ann said as she pulled me out of my daydreams.

"Yes, I am thoughtful these days. I'm wondering what the hell I'm doing here and whether I belong. I don't feel tough enough, Sarah Ann, and right now I wonder if it isn't masochistic to stay."

She saw right through me. "You must have looped ME. You know a lot of people are hurting right now."

I hadn't thought about that part too much. I'd only been thinking about me.

"Remember," she said, "what you told me in October. Your friend Holly said it. They break you down into little pieces and build you up again. We were broken down; now we are in pieces. Listen, I know some people who looped three exams. Three."

"Three? Three is me, Sarah Ann. See how dumb I am! Do you still want to know me?"

Sarah Ann looked a bit sheepish. I didn't mean to embarrass her, nor she me. We were both on the edge of what we considered our emotional cliff and I knew it when she lifted her head and whispered, "Listen, I've told you before, but I must repeat it. You're very important to me. You understand so many things that I don't. You make connections between events and interpret things with your intuition that impress me each and every day. You must value yourself for those things because they are much more important than mastering ME or Control.

"And I have something else to say. I've not told anyone

because I'm too uncomfortable. But I looped OB and came close in Control."

"You're kidding," I said.

It hit me like a wallop. Sarah Ann had that seemingly natural intelligence that comes with good training in analytical subjects. She didn't study very hard, not nearly as hard as I did with my four to six hours a night. And to Kate, Sarah Ann was a miracle because she only studied three or so hours while Kate worked well past midnight. But Kate and I knew that Sarah Ann didn't have to study. Whenever she raised her hand in class, she said something very smart. We loved her for it.

"But, Sarah Ann, it's not possible. It's just not possible," I stammered.

Control had seemed so easy to her. And OB; OB was as easy as they come.

"It's hard to admit. I've never failed at anything. I went to talk to Bob Murphy already. He was wonderful. And now I have some idea what he was looking for. You see, I never had to write before. You don't learn that in engineering school."

She went on, and even though it was me she was talking to, I could tell it was hard for her to say, "In Control I got into the exam and started to do the questions and I knew I really didn't understand. Somewhere along the line I missed some important stuff on variances because I just didn't get it. So you see it's not only you who loops the exams."

We were walking back to campus now. I felt one thousand times better than I had earlier that day, and I told Sarah Ann, "It was hard to tell me—but it meant so much and I appreciate it. It's really hard to fail and feel out of it when you've gone along your whole life accomplishing each goal, one after another. Thanks so much, Sarah Ann, and congratulations again to you and Jack."

Somehow our conversation settled me down and made me ready to deal with my situation. Later in the evening I dug out the office number for the counseling office. I decided I'd drop by the next day to talk to a counselor. And for the rest of the night I played music and called friends, feeling as though I had turned one of those funny invisible corners in life. The landscape was changing all around me and perhaps I would change with it.

The next day at lunch break I did go to counseling. It was wonderful even though I was in pain for the whole hour. I talked and told Kathy, the school therapist, exactly how I felt.

"Miserable. I'm too sensitive or not tough or something. Sometimes in class the discussion is so cut and dried, as though we were simply in a vocational training program, getting each ticket punched along the way."

Kathy listened for an hour. She then said I was welcome to come and see her at any time. "Before you go, let me share some of my experiences as a counselor at HBS. It's like no other place I've ever been. You have to look at yourself honestly and ask, 'What did I expect when I came here?' This is not a place for poets or philosophers. It's not a place for renaissance people to be born or nurtured. It is a training ground for strategists, for optimists, for planners, for goal-oriented thinkers.

"Some of the students I've seen over the years have tried to change the HBS process. It didn't work. They only clashed with the school at every turn. It's a very big system, a well-supported, well-oiled machine that's much bigger than you. And from its point of view, it doesn't need you.

"The students who have allowed themselves to fit around this process are the ones who have done okay. They accept

Harvard for what it is and try to be themselves in spite of it. Do you recall how well the militarily trained students in your section are doing? They're probably getting through without batting an eye. Think about what that means for you, with your background. You're being much too hard on yourself to expect to be anywhere but where you are right now, here in my office."

I drank in every word. I wanted to stay in her office for another hour, or forever, just because it felt so good to be understood. And I knew what she said was true. It even shocked me to hear her mention poets because I fancied myself a poet, writing here and there when it pleased me, giving poems to friends as gifts. I hadn't written a poem since I had come to school in September.

Why didn't everyone go to counseling, I wondered as I headed out of her door and into the snowy courtyard. Well, not everyone needed it, I reasoned; nor can everyone share his or her pain and life and seek support. I was relieved to be just myself, a woman, trained in psychology and not in the military.

The Production and Operations Management exam was two days off. Rumor had it that the exam had been scheduled for the last day before vacation so that we wouldn't leave early. The school couldn't tolerate students skipping classes, we knew. Duke Moore said as much when he ended our last POM class early with a short lecture. It was the first talk we had had from any professor that could be labeled fatherly advice. Duke had become a guru of sorts to the class because so many of us felt he was an excellent professor. He had the remarkable skill of knowing when to laugh and ease the pressure.

"Please take time this holiday to care for people you've ignored these past few months," he began.

We all laughed good-naturedly even though there was some squirming in our seats, too. As a section we knew of at least one separation and many strained relationships. He continued, "Now, I've talked to most of you in my office and I know that a lot of you have doubts about the program and about your education here. The faculty believes it's the best in the nation. We've looked at the MBA schedule from every different angle. We believe that the training you go through here will equip you to be excellent general managers, perhaps the finest in the world. The people who come to recruit on campus tell us so, and we know it from our graduates. Have a great vacation, and since there is a break now in the POM schedule, I won't see you until the spring."

I wasn't so sure about Duke's judgment on general managers and what made good ones. But then, what did I recognize in his voice—kindness? concern?

Well maybe, I thought, just maybe . . . it will be downhill from here.

4

CHANGES

There was no doubt that there were changes taking place in me. On Christmas Eve my parents arrived safely in a snowstorm with half of my family, to the great relief of the rest of us. I was the first to greet them.

"Did you have a profitable trip?" I said warmly.

"A profitable trip?" My mother tilted her head, narrowed her eyes, and looked at me with her familiar intense stare. "What do you mean by that?"

I didn't know what I meant by it. It had just popped out. And they teased me for days. Was this their daughter, the one who marched in Washington, D.C., against the Vietnam War? The one who brought home Joan Baez albums in 1966, when everyone else was listening to the Beach Boys? They had gingerly accommodated themselves to my activist lifestyle as we all grew older together. Now what? They asked if I was going to become one of those Yippee-Hippies-turned-business tycoons.

I brushed off their questions but privately registered their concern. I was worried about it too. My conversations with Kathy in the counseling office came back to me as I rested over the holidays and then moved my possessions to my new apartment, located on a quiet street in Cambridge. Yes, Harvard Business School was very big. It was bigger than I was. There were many things about it that I didn't like, things like the work load and the sadistic people who forced it on us, producing harried, insecure people. But I hadn't come to Harvard to change the place. I had come to learn how to run a business, how to be a manager, how to plan strategically.

I took the vacation for myself and didn't open a book for ten days. Instead, I planned my next month and wrote down the steps I had to take to get through it. At the end of January were final exams in ME, Control, OB. We wouldn't have finals in POM or Marketing until the end of the school year, because we didn't pick up these courses again until the spring.

My first step in planning for the finals was to choose between ME and Control. Since I had looped both midterms I knew I would have to do something extra to assure myself a Sat in both of them. Before the vacation, I had gone to talk to Kirk about my grade and he had suggested that I not try to do too much in January. "It's a hard month, with your new courses beginning and all," he'd said.

By now I knew enough to take him seriously, and when I thought about it, the choice was easy. In ME we had begun regression analysis in early December. Regression analysis is the art of forecasting an unknown based on information currently known.

For example, if a manager was planning to open a new store in a suburban mall, what demographics would be most important to predict the store's sales: traffic on the highway; the number of TV sets in the surrounding town., or perhaps the amount of disposable income per capita? These few sentences described everything I knew about regression analysis, and I knew there was much more that I should know because we would study it for a month and it would be worth half of the final exam grade.

For the last three weeks of ME class we would study linear programming. It sounded dense and mysterious. Could I learn enough about linear programming in three weeks to answer the other half of my exam? I wondered. No, I doubted it. And even though I planned to purchase a computer as soon as I was out of school, I knew I'd hardly ever need regression analysis and linear programming working with the small businesses my company served. I resolved to do my best, but not a whole lot, to get ready for ME.

That being decided, I thought about Control. The logical action was to hire a tutor, which the counseling office could help me do. With a tutor once or twice a week, I could get questions answered in a much more direct fashion than I could in the classroom.

By the evening before the first day back at school I felt prepared, even if I wasn't all that rested. It had taken most of the last week to move. But even though I was physically tired, it was worth it to sit on my own furniture, eat a dinner I had cooked for myself, and listen to some women's music on my stereo.

At seven o'clock on Sunday night I pulled out my next day's assignments and cases. I was amazingly blasé to have waited so long. My classes the next day were ME, Control, and Finance—a tough trio. But by now I'd developed a pattern in doing cases and it didn't take me nearly as long to complete them. My approach was to read through the case first, then read the questions, and then the case again, analyzing it as I moved along. The notes I took now were more specifically aimed at the questions than they had been in the fall, when I was almost rewriting the cases in an effort to get on top of the material.

In Control we were beginning a short segment on takeover attempts and how to account for them on the purchasing company's books. It struck me as odd that in our class discussions on mergers and acquisitions we never took the position of the taken over, only that of the aggressor.

In ME we were deep into regression analysis, using it to make competitive bids. I smiled to myself as I read through the assignment:

> *Class #41, January 5*
>
> Read: J. L. Hayes & Sons (pp. 403–410)
>
> Prepare:
> 1. Analyze the information contained in J. L. Hayes & Sons—Regression Analysis Supplement. Note that some of the slides involve the variable spread which is defined to be Hayes' price minus Continental's bid. Select an appropriate probability distribution for Continental's bid or the spread.
>
> 2. Determine a bid for J. L. Hayes & Sons. Each student should be prepared to submit a bid for *Hayes* at the beginning of the class.
>
> 3. (Optional) Use the AQD regression package to develop a probabilistic forecast for Continental's bid. Data for the case are in permanent workfile 1HAYS (access as 1HAYS/L) in the HBS data library. Variables are:
>
> 1. issue number (1, 2, 3, . . .)
> 2. par value (27.5, 16.0, . . .)
> 3. Moody rating, with 5 correspond to Aaa, 4 for Aa, 3 for A, 2 for Baa and 1 for Ba.

4. number of bidders (4, 5, . . .)
5. Hayes price (99.036, 103.356, . . .)
6. Continental's bid (97.97, 102.152, . . .)

I struggled to determine a reasonable bid for J. L. Hayes, but knew I'd have a hard time defending it if I was called on to open the class. I had made the right choice to let this course go.

Turning to Finance, I felt an old, familiar sensation as I read through the first assignment. The feeling was the same as I had had in September—panic at the expectation that I should know what to do, how to do Finance for the very first class.

Finance was fundamental to our education as managers. A primary goal of the course was to teach students how to use financial techniques to analyze a company. These techniques included cash budgeting; pro forma statements; ratio analysis; discounted cash flow; and risk analysis. Other goals were to acquaint us with the financial markets in which firms sought funds—such as the bond, stock, and money markets. We'd also learn finance theory and have a chance to make investment decisions in various environments.

But none of this was clear as I turned to the first case. It was Browning Lumber and we were asked to determine how much money Mr. Browning would need to fund his company for the next year. Then we were asked to map out a way for him to get the money. Should he borrow more or sell stock? I sat and thought about it. Yes, it was the same old feeling. How can I know how to do this before I know how to do it? But then a different feeling arose, and it came out of things I remembered from the Control midterm. I put down some rough numbers to make up an income statement and determine how much money he would have as net profit. He needed more in order to grow. Should he sell stock or borrow? I didn't know, but I had done enough for the night. And I was even a little pleased with myself. Maybe I did know something, after all.

The next day I wasn't called on to offer my bid in Managerial Economics. I'd never been called on in ME and that suited me just fine. I recalled the last day of classes before vacation, when Joe had called on Carol Mathias to open. She wasn't prepared and Joe had looked angry when he said, "Just because it's the last day is no excuse. You should be prepared every day."

Carol had been struggling all semester. She was very smart, but she was young, too. At twenty-one she was the youngest in the class, and it was hard for her to assert herself with everyone around her seeming to know so much more. At that moment tears had welled up in her eyes, and she had left the room until the class was over. But today Joe called on Stan Hooper, the best student in ME class, and I realized that would probably be Horst's strategy for the last few weeks. Now he would determine who should get E's and who should get Sats by giving the better students a chance to show what they knew.

Finance class began with silence as the professor walked in. I was struck by his age and size. He couldn't be more than twenty-five, I thought, and he's a small man. Wow, that takes guts, to try and teach us with such an age and size disadvantage. His name was Edward Stein; we all waited for more but he didn't say anything. He started right in by calling on my former roommate, Pat Worth, to open. Many of us couldn't take our eyes off Edward. He looked fragile in front of us. And it wasn't just his size that I noticed, but the feeling that he was an intruder into our classroom.

We were Section D. Our six professors and the eighty-five of us left were like a unit. We partied together, we played sports together, we laughed in class to ease the tension, we all held our breaths when someone made a mistake. We'd had a spellbinding, unbroken four months of work together. And here, with no other introduction but "Edward Stein," it was all changed. We had learned in OB that within a corporation people develop a set of behaviors which define them as a group. We labeled the behavior corporate culture. We learned also how to identify and define the corporate culture in the firms we interviewed with. If we understood the corporate culture, then we could work with it and not against it.

Well, Section D had its corporate culture. We had a reputation for being a polite, hard-working section, not given to much competition or aggression. In some ways, that might change as we were introduced into our new courses and had to deal with new professors leading our discussions. We would have a WSA lunch that week, and I planned to bring up the topic.

Some of the Section D WSA members didn't come to the lunch on Thursday because there was a computer exercise for ME that day which took up the lunch hour of some students. We were a small group, but even so it felt good to sit around and talk about how we felt about being back in school. Kate was there and so were Sheryl Shaw, Susan Mantero, Sarah Ann, Danielle, and I. We started to talk about our vacation. Susan spoke first and we all laughed with her when she told us that Michael Mitchell had come up to introduce himself during the first class back. He had obviously thought she was a visitor.

"He was so embarrassed when I said, 'Michael, it's me, Susan.'"

We all agreed that she looked like a different woman. Susan had lost thirty pounds during the first semester, and by the end of it, all of her clothes hung about her like extra baggage. She had had no time to shop for the first few months. Over the holiday she had bought new clothes and gotten a permanent. She said she was tired but feeling much better now that she had had a chance to get back to eating right.

Danielle said that she, too, came back from the holiday with a whole new sense of herself. She was another person at family gatherings, arguing about issues and no longer resigning herself to listening to discussions. She even found herself thinking about persuasion techniques we had learned in Management Communications.

Sheryl Shaw lived in Boston and had gone to a singles bar over the holiday. We looked at her with our eyes open wide as she told us what happened.

"Don't go to a singles bar and say you go to HBS," she said. "It's a disaster. I should have known better; I had a warning from a woman friend who graduated HBS in the late sixties. She said the hardest part of the whole experience was dealing with the male students. They were brutal. They didn't know how to handle the women, so they just left them out. My friend ended up feeling like a pariah and now I have an idea why."

She continued, "I was at Daisy Buchanan's—you know, the bar in Boston. I was enjoying a drink with a friend when this good-looking man came over to our table and introduced himself. It wasn't long before he started bragging about his job and how important he was in it. Then he said what really kept him busy was that he went to Harvard Business School on the side."

"You can guess what I replied," Sheryl said. "I said, 'Oh, what section?' And he looked blankly past me and said, 'Section? What Section?' and of course I said, 'A, B, C, D.' 'Well D,' he replied, 'Section D.'"

We all burst into laughter. We loved this story.

"'D? I'm in Section D at Harvard Business School,' I said. 'I've never seen you there.' Well, he backed away from the table and sputtered and kicked all the way across the room, defending himself as he went. He said, 'Oh well, I've got to have my classes taped, I'm so busy at work I can't get away. Ah, see you around.'"

We were rolling across the floor by now and so was Sheryl. "But do you know the hardest thing about it?" she said. "My friend, who watched the whole thing, wasn't laughing at all. He said that I'd been hard on him, that I was an unmerciful woman. Now, you tell me where we're supposed to fit, with all our brains and aspirations."

It took us a while to settle down after Sheryl's story. When we did, I said that I had had time to think about things over the holidays, too. "I found myself carrying my calendar around with me. I had to write down everything I wanted to do because there is so much other information in my head now I was afraid I'd forget my plans. There on my list were: give presents to Mom, call Joyce, write thank you to B. J. Even the most common things I'd do out of habit before, I had to write down. Worse yet, I moved into my apartment over the holiday and last week absentmindedly shut the door to the basement, locking my landlady in the laundry room. She was steaming mad because she was caught down there for an hour, but all I could do was apologize and blame it on the pressure.

"It's as if I were programmed or something. And in the first Finance class the other day, I was unnerved because our schedule, our class, was so interrupted by the invasion of a new professor. I resented it."

Kate looked at me knowingly. "Yes, there are a lot of changes," she said.

"Things we don't even realize. Like the way the women don't talk in class much anymore. And the way I see people starting to compete. In ME this morning, did you catch the way the whole class laughed when Joe Horst slipped and almost fell on a piece of gravel on the floor? It was as if we all were daring him not to lose his balance instead of reaching out to help him stand up."

Our meeting broke up with sobering thoughts of these changes passing between us like a heavy weight. It was good, at least, to sit around together and get some relief from the pressures.

The next week sped by. There was a lot of work to be done, just as Kirk Cranston had warned me before the holiday. I had a group assignment to do outside of class time with a team, which consisted of three men and me. It was an OB exercise on the Glass Works Division at Corning Glass. The section was divided into teams, and some of us played the role of the new chief executive officer of Corning Glass, while some of us were outside consultants, hired to analyze organizational problems in the Glass Works Division.

I didn't like group assignments. We had had a few in the fall in MC and they had conjured up the same unease I had felt with the study group. With group assignments I had to face squarely my lack of interest in competing with other students and it unnerved me. And these assignments soaked up hours of time, while we still were expected to do three cases a night. For the OB exercise, our team were consultants and we were pitted against three other consultant teams. We were scheduled to report to "Tom McAvoy," in reality a group of our section mates. We'd be judged on our ability to analyze the problems in Glass Works and communicate our analysis to the judging team.

Stan Hooper was in our group, along with two men I hardly knew—Ramon Pires and Ron Watts. Ramon was from Portugal, and Ron was from the West Coast, an accounting major. Ramon and Stan were both engineers. When we met outside the classroom it was strange at first, because we had to work out everything—a way to work together, a structure for our analysis, and a format for our presentation. We had only a week to do it.

We met three or four times, and I was surprised at how much I could contribute to our work together. At first I was not very helpful, especially when we nailed down our overall business strategy, because we had to make a choice between recommending that Glass Works be abandoned as a business opportunity or invested in heavily with the purpose of turning it around. To make the choice, we needed to project the division's market growth and sales potential. I didn't have the ability to make the necessary connections yet between production capability and market share. Somehow Stan and Ramon understood it, but they reached opposite conclusions. Stan thought we should recommend divesting the division because the future for Glass Works was bleak. Ramon said no, we should put money into it and our recommendations should deal with necessary organizational changes in order to invest successfully. We decided to invest, simply because Ron knew that Tom McAvoy, the current chief executive officer of Corning, used to be the head of the Glass Works Division—and thus we knew that the company had invested in real life and been successful at it.

When it came time to map out our presentation, I offered my opinion freely. It was uncomfortable, almost as though I weren't trained or psychologically able to sit across the table from two engineers and an accountant and give them my point of view. But I did and we pieced together our presentation, each of us planning to speak for ten minutes or so, giving the judging panel a chance to ask questions. My role was to suggest change in "Tom's" style of managing. He didn't delegate enough and he'd have to if the division was going to grow.

By the time our team presented our conclusions to the judging panel, I was ready with a strategy. I moved up close to them and spoke as personally as I could. I looked them right in the eyes and told them that if Tom McAvoy wanted a successful division he had to clarify objectives, delegate responsibility, and hold people accountable for results.

Apparently it worked, because the judges decided we were the best consultants and they cited my personal approach as a major reason for our success. I should have felt elated . . . but I didn't. I felt—what? . . . a strange kind of embarrassment. It was a creepy feeling, one that told me, sure you know how to play the game now; you want to compete and win just like everybody else.

There were two undercurrents that seemed to move in the class now, and I felt them keenly. On the surface we were still Section D, loyal to each other and supportive of our individual differences. But under this there was a great deal of teasing and a lot of jockeying for position. We were competing with each other and at the same time developing a fierce comformity, as though if we conformed we'd be in a better position to compete.

The pressure to conform came in subtle ways. One small outward sign was the way in which people dressed. At first only one or two men in the class wore their Izod shirts under their oxford shirts. Now a half dozen or more regularly came to class in this latest prep outfit. And while before the holiday only one student wore a scarf around his neck in class, now both men and women often had their scarves on all day. There was some inner need to be alike, to look alike.

I saw this a little more clearly in the activities of some of the student clubs. There were dozens of them on campus—most career-oriented, like the Marketing Club, the Finance Club, and the Management Consulting Club. But some were support groups for their members, like the Afro-American

Student Union, the Women's Student Association, and the Gay Students Association. I was amazed and impressed to watch WSA. Its members worked very hard to fit in, to have the women on campus taken seriously by the faculty and the students. They implemented a fantastic effort to get course reviews scheduled and printed up for each midterm and final.

The Gay Students Association was a very active but closeted group. Its members were not interested in advertising themselves to anyone, because the managements of most corporations are homophobic. They wouldn't recruit or hire gay students, and once hired, if a graduate let it be known that he or she was gay, it was cause for dismissal or the end of a promising career. Even though GSA members were not public, some still sought conformity in the Harvard image. This came home to me when talking with a HBS graduate of a few years before who had founded GSA. The group that banded together could not call itself "gay": it was the "Club for Alternative Executive Life Styles."

Black students were not exempt from a need to fit in. When the club leadership recently reviewed candidates to elect a new president, they had a hard time considering one young woman who was eager to serve. As a friend put it to me, people knew she was a member of GSA, and they didn't think a gay would look good as the president of the Afro-American Student Union.

Pressure to conform came from the professors and the classroom too. One example flashed at me when I read the comments on my POM exam in mid-January. Duke had graded me with a Sat "too close to a failure to be easy going," he had written on my booklet. The exam wasn't a hard one, I thought, but maybe that was because I wasn't under the same kind of pressure in December that I felt before Thanksgiving. It also may have been the fact that the protagonist in the case was a woman, the third case of the two hundred I'd read that was about a woman. It also was about a product I understood, soft contact lenses. We were asked to plan out a strategy for Nancy Lang, who was Sof-optics' director of marketing and who was faced with growing sales and production bottlenecks. A key element in the correct strategy was to recognize that as director of marketing she didn't have authority over the production process. She could just recommend. Because she had too many responsibilities, my strategy had been for her to consider splitting her job and hiring another person to share the work load.

Duke Moore disagreed. He asked me in his notes whether I would ever consider splitting my job in real life. I thought long and hard about the point. I liked this professor, the course, and wanted to learn as much as I could, but I couldn't agree with the implication of his question. Yes, I would consider splitting my job; in fact I had done it. And Harvard was wrong to try and make us think that we always had to go after power for ourselves whenever we found the opportunity. Sometimes power can be gained by improving the company in some way that doesn't affect one personally. For example, if Nancy Lang lost some power in splitting her job, she could gain much more by being responsible for improving Sof-Optics' efficiency and taking credit for the resulting new profits.

I discussed my discomfort about conforming with Sarah Ann and Kate. They knew what I meant.

"Remember when we did that résumé and letter-writing exercise in MC last fall?" Sarah Ann asked.

I remembered that we had been required to write our résumé in the one-page Harvard style for the first-year résumé book. We had written letters under pseudonyms and been criticized by other students on our résumés and our letter-writing abilities.

"Well," Sarah Ann said. "One student wrote back on my résumé that I shouldn't put down that I got my master's magna cum laude from my Texas school. It didn't mean anything, he said, to those who would be interviewing me. The only thing that meant anything was distinction at a well-known school."

"How awful," Kate said, "for all of us to be expected to look just like the East Coast Harvard man."

"Which reminds me of a funny story a friend from another section told me this morning," I said. "It's about how even the professors don't quite see us as individuals."

I looked at them, knowing they'd remember the case.

"Do you recall when we did probability assessments in ME? In Section G, the professor decided to demonstrate how most statistics fall into the bell curve and he did so by taking down each student's height and putting it on a unisex grid. He aimed to show how 'average' all heights are together. When he got to my friend Casse, she called out five feet eight inches and he put that in the medium column. She stared at him, speechless, and later told me, 'Think about it, Fran. Before coming here, I was a tall woman; now that I'm at Harvard, I'm a medium-sized man!'"

We laughed for a while as we did often when we talked about school—it was a healthy way to release the everyday tension.

Kate spoke what was on my mind when she started in a serious vein, "The scary thing is that I'm right there with everyone else. I think I'm different, but I'm not. Today I watched Patrick Jones—you know, the Brit on the skydeck who never talks. I realized today that he has never raised his hand to speak voluntarily. What's wrong with him, I wondered. What makes him think he doesn't have to contribute?"

"Yes, I know what you mean," I said. "It's very hard, impossible really, not to resent him for not playing it Harvard's way, talking like the rest of us, I can't accept him for what he is."

"And," Sarah Ann chimed in, "the really hard thing to know is whether we were all like this before we came here or whether we're beginning to conform to the norm. Whether we're finished being broken into little pieces and are now being built up again."

"Gee whiz," I said. "Where *am* I in all this? *Who* am I in this process?"

I went right home and wrote a poem. It wasn't the best one I'd ever written, but a sweeping sensation of relief came over me as I typed out the words. I wasn't as changed as I thought. After all, I could still write poems. I brought it in to the school newspaper, the *Harbus News*, and while I was there I signed up to be the events editor of the paper. The editor and the publisher were both women, recently elected to their positions, and I wanted to help them out. Diane Gallagher, the editor, was pleased to publish my poem, and when it appeared the next week, quite a few male students told me it expressed their feelings too. I read it over again:

"Weeks Bridge '81"

I'm sucking wind,
taking it in,
breathing hard,
pushing to find
that piece of me
which is playful,
that roll in the
hay full.
I'm losing control
and my soul is dry.

Where's the time for me?

The poetry;
the rhythm I cherish,
that voice and shy smile.
I've got this long mile
hanging over my head.
My soul feels dead.

Standing here in terror
I gape at the moon.
I have no time to view
her fully, like I like
to do.

Sometimes this place
makes me feel like crying.
But I hide it in sighing
and buying
time for my future.

There was no symbolism in it. It was as stark and simple as it could be. So be it, I thought; it was just how I felt.

"Can we all get through with no one hitting the screen?" I asked.

There was an uncomfortable movement in our seats. It was Monday, February 2, and we were meeting as a section after classes were over. The education rep, Rick Cabot, stood before us explaining the grading system again so that we'd all clearly understand it before finals. The Managerial Economics exam was on Saturday, the Control and OB exams on Monday and Tuesday. As before, we had no time to study; we had classes and cases through Friday afternoon.

The screen hadn't been as ominous a presence before. It's not that we had ignored it; it just hadn't been as imminent as it was now. The screen was a euphemism for the process which brought students before the Academic Standards Board after first year grades were published. The screen got its name literally; in the registrar's office there was a computer video display terminal on which appeared the names of students who got eight credits of loops in first year. Their names "hit the screen," and thus they were subject to dismissal from the school.

Some students were asked to take a year off; others were simply asked to leave. The process of review and dismissal took place over the summer between first and second year, so it was tucked neatly out of most students' view. But in late January, with nearly three hundred fifty cases behind us, the screen was a menacing reality for probably thirty percent of the class. It deeply concerned another forty percent. The rest of the class, the top students, worried themselves over honors.

The screen worried both Kate and me. On the face of it, it seemed ridiculous. We did our work every night. We talked regularly, though not every day, in class. The pressure that made us worry came from not knowing how well we were doing or how much we knew. And since we had looped a few midterms, we were scared that we'd loop our finals too. Talking in class was half our grade, exams the other half. If we looped exams, would what we said in class pull us through? Not according to our grades on class participation. Even though we talked what seemed a lot to me, it wasn't good enough according to our Sat minus and Low Pass plus class-participation grade.

Our class meeting was meant to reassure us.

"Only five to ten percent of the section gets Low Passes," Rick said, continuing his pep talk.

But I still wanted to know the answer to my question. Could we all get through without any of us hitting the screen?

I knew the implication of my question. It was that some of us would have to take loops voluntarily to save the others. Because we had ten courses and eighty-five students, it meant that eight hundred fifty grades were given out. If ten percent of them must be Low Pass, that meant that one Low Pass each would mean no one would get four and fail.

Stan Hooper raised his hand and made obvious what we all knew was implied. "The school would frown on that effort," he said.

But I thought to myself sarcastically, yes, but wouldn't we be proving what a good management team we are if we could manipulate HBS into letting us all get through? But I knew that the competitive urge was too great—no one would flunk a course to demonstrate that kind of teamwork.

Danielle Murray jumped in. "I'll volunteer to take the loop in Control."

We all laughed and understood how she felt. Most of us, including the CPAs, were nervous about Control. Kirk Cranston had held a review session the previous Saturday, and he had geared it to those who thought they were in the bottom third of the class. At least eighty percent of the seats were filled at 9 A.M., when he walked in. He couldn't hide the look of dismay on his face when he saw all of us; he knew then how insecure we all were.

Our laughter moved us away from the uncomfortable moment, and the subject was not mentioned again. But I couldn't help wondering what was so radical about trying to help one another out. Wasn't that what good corporate management was about, in part? Just because the school assumed that three or four out of eighty-five had to be dismissed didn't mean that we had to agree. We didn't sign a contract with the school whereby we accepted those terms. By late January I had talked with and gotten to know each and every person in my section. Some people I liked more than others, but I cared about each one and about their lives. It bothered me to think that some of us would put all that work into first year and then not be allowed to continue.

By now I was walking home, over the bridge and through Harvard Square. I lived a mile from campus, and I loved the walk each day. It was so cold; it woke me up in the mornings and in the afternoons got me going again after sitting in my seat all day. My walks, like my runs, helped me to sort through the day and process my emotions.

But today's walk made me uneasy. Whenever I got to thinking about the screen, my mind stopped as if I were against a brick wall. I couldn't push beyond it to new ground, although Rick's talk changed things some because now it was more real. Final exams in three subjects before the week was over. I knew I could get a Sat in OB, but if I looped Control and ME, I was in hot water. That meant if I looped two out of the other three—Marketing, POM, or Finance—I was out. Unfortunately, it didn't seem like a far-fetched possibility.

On the other hand, if I looped three, not four, courses I was safe and other classmates would have that much less pressure on them. This train of thought was more akin to the opinion I had expressed at our class meeting. But it didn't do any good to care about my classmates, I realized. The only concern I had was to get through myself. The school's system was set up so that we had to compete with one another. In fact, the way the game was played was to do the very best you could and worry about yourself first.

I shook my head as I walked. Even the cold New England air couldn't clear away my dismay about this aspect of the system. But I realized that it wasn't such an unusual concept for most people. The school probably selected those who were most likely to compete, perhaps even students who would relish the competition.

Hennig and Jardim came to mind. Years ago, in *The Managerial Woman*, they had spelled out the handicap that many women in business suffered from. Women didn't know team sports and didn't know how to play the games that men learn from the time they are toddlers. The essence of it is to learn competition. But even though I knew that team sports were an important training ground, it was unsettling to realize that I was expected to compete not as a part of a team, but on my own behalf.

Perhaps this was the source of the stereotype of the Harvard MBA, someone who is aggressively pursuing his or her own goals, disregarding the needs of others. Memories about my image of the school flooded back to me when I considered this. The first memory to come to mind was of a stranger who had called me late one evening the previous summer.

"Hi," he'd said, "my name is Jack Stark. I'm a Harvard alum. I tried to call you at your office for the past three nights but no one answered. What's going on at your office that no one answers the phone at six-thirty?"

Not being accustomed to such a rude introduction by a total stranger, I was taken off guard and stammered, "Well, ah, well, I don't know; guess it's hot in D.C. in July and people go home early," I said.

"It can't be a very hard working office," he continued. "I'm calling to invite you to a party for new admits. Congratulations, by the way. It's Friday night at the Potomac Yacht Club. Love to see you there."

He hung up, leaving me feeling defensive. Why should I be explaining my company's reasonable office hours to a stranger, I'd wondered.

But more to the point, I recalled wondering what I was getting myself into if Jack Stark was typical of the students at Harvard. Another memory came to mind, one which reminded me that the pressure was felt by the faculty as well as the students. It wasn't a pleasant thought. In a conversation with a woman who had graduated a few years ago, I had heard that her OB professor had committed suicide right in the middle of the year. Was it because of the pressure and the competition?

And what about that awful incident over Turkey Bingo? Turkey Bingo was the name of a student game that apparently cropped up every year. Some students organized it by drawing out a matrix with twenty students' names, one in each box. The students with their names in a box had to raise their hands to be recognized. The game was like regular bingo in that whenever a string of names was checked off vertically or horizontally, a player was ready to win. But to win, a student had to raise his or her hand, be recognized, and in the middle of commenting on the case recite the saying of the day. The saying was always ridiculous, something like "Professor, I know you are smart and I am dumb, but in this case our positions reverse . . ."

The first day Section D played Turkey Bingo there was a crowd around the organizer, Ron Watts. I didn't play but I was amused by the game. It was just like us. To play cost a quarter and the winner got the pool. Bingo sheets were done on the school's computer and word processor. By the second class that day, most of us not playing the game had forgotten about it. But all of a sudden in the middle of ME class Richard Travis, in his comment on Hudepohl Brewing Company, said something utterly unintelligible. Then he jumped up and said, "I won, I won Turkey Bingo!"

Joe Horst, in his usual way, rolled his eyes upward and smiled. But we were all mortified, for Joe and for Richard.

After class that day, Ron Watts apologized to us. And he, in the coldest way possible, disassociated himself from Richard's outburst. It was a very painful moment, made more so by Richard's profuse apology to the class.

What's so wrong about it, I thought. We're all under so much pressure to win, to get ahead. Why be so hard on Richard for losing himself to the moment?

Competition sometimes took the peculiar form of not helping one another. In the past week, two incidents had brought this home to me. On Tuesday Sheryl Shaw gave her Management Communications speech. Sheryl had become, by now, an honors candidate, since she spoke frequently in class and had a solid handle on nearly every subject. She was a scientist by training and she certainly had a knack for case discussion. But on the day of her MC speech, she started to talk, then hesitated once or twice. It was an interesting talk about new advertising phenomena, but it was obvious from the thick pile of audio visuals that she had too much material for her five-minute time limit. Right in the middle of a sentence she stammered and flushed red. She looked quickly at Margaret Price, our professor, who suggested that she go on. But she only spoke a few words and then froze and couldn't look up or down. She just stood there in the pit of the classroom with eighty-five students and a professor staring at her for what seemed like minutes but probably was thirty seconds or so.

I raised my hand; she couldn't see it. I raised my voice but it sounded squeaky, as though I were afraid to speak up.

"Sheryl, do you mind if I ask a question? Where do you think this field will be in a few years?" I asked.

She looked up gratefully and answered my questions easily, then went on to finish her speech with no delay.

When the class broke, she and others came over to thank me, to congratulate me for speaking up. So many others had wanted to do something but hadn't known what.

I didn't feel like a heroine. Truthfully, it didn't take courage to save someone who was twisting slowly in the wind. Why wasn't it easy for more of us to rescue Sheryl, and why weren't we developing skills to do that—skills general managers need to help others do their jobs.

Instead, we were under pressure to compete with one another. Like earlier today, when Stan Hooper walked with me into the administration building. He held the first door open for me. Since I was ahead of him, I held the second for him. He balked; he couldn't walk through. He put his arm over my head and held the door even though it meant he had to step out of my way while I eased around him.

"Come now, Stan," I said, "surely I can open the door for you."

"It's a habit I learned in the military," he said. "I always open the door for my people."

I gave him a good, long, hard, mean look as he walked off down the hall, totally unaware of what he'd said. Since when have I become "his people"? How tiring to have to rush to be the first to open doors or to have to step out of the way. Why can't I just open a door if I am first to it?

But competition wasn't limited to my classmates. I had developed a healthy dose of it myself, and it troubled me as I ended the walk home and headed up my stairway to prepare for the next day's cases.

It struck me first when Michael Mitchell and I were eating lunch. Or rather it struck him, I thought, because he sat with his jaw open when he asked me whether I'd heard from Melanie or Joanne, the women who had left school before midterms the previous fall. No, I hadn't heard from them; I didn't know them that well.

Michael said he missed them. "I liked their sense of humor," he said, "even though they were quiet in class."

I looked at him and replied, "Well if they weren't doing

well I wished they had stayed. Now who's going to get loops in the tough classes?"

Michael stared at me, choking on his food. He didn't say anything, but I read his mind: who indeed, Fran Henry? You should be ashamed of yourself.

I was. But I was also hoping to get through Harvard Business School.

5

PLAYING THE GAME

I've written it in my journal and now I go back in disbelief and read the words: "I love Finance." My expression isn't a lie and it isn't forced. It's Tuesday, February 17, and perhaps for the first time I appreciate what I'm learning. It happened quite suddenly.

Yesterday was Monday, Washington's Birthday, and we had the day off. I decided to go through my stack of *Wall Street Journal*s, which had piled up in the last few weeks. I was accustomed to picking up that paper and browsing through it for things I could relate to. Most of the time I just read the first page. It was a shock to discover that I understood article after article, and because of it, I sat and read for the entire afternoon.

It was exhilarating; I understood when I read about pending federal tax legislation and the tax effect of accelerated depreciation. I read with fascination about long-term bonds and the uncertainty of interest rates which made them a risky but attractive investment. And I read of an unsuccessful merger between two companies and the resulting run up and then drop in the target company's stock price.

When I felt that exhilaration, I knew that for me Finance was what business school was all about. In Marketing I was learning techniques to analyze and sell products and services, but the basic orientation I already understood. Good marketing simply required a heightened sensitivity to what the outside world is telling you, and these skills are just the ones I got from my training in psychology. Production and Operations Management was very useful in terms of knowing what the production process is all about, but I doubted that I would be involved in large-scale manufacturing, and I'd probably never use learning curves or EOQs or need to know cycle times. Organizational Behavior and Management Communications were courses I enjoyed because they gave me time to breathe in between the hard work in the other courses, but I already felt comfortable with the course content. In Managerial Economics I learned things that enabled me to make big business decisions "by the numbers." I doubted whether I would make many of my small business decisions with ME tools, but I was grateful to the course for my introduction into the world of computers, and even though I never had time to use them, I did watch them working in Baker Library.

Control and Finance remained. I valued Control much more now because I could see how each subject we dealt with in Control was used in Finance. As I sat reading my journal and the entries I had made since September, I realized I was at a loss then to know what value all of my hard work would have other than getting my ticket, the MBA, at the other end. Finally it made some sense. Finance would help me understand interest rates, stock prices, and investment decisions. Not only were they things that I didn't understand before school, but they could also be immediately applied in my business.

I was enamored with Finance, but unfortunately my feelings didn't translate that well into the classroom. It didn't make what I was learning any easier, just more satisfying. We dealt with new tools every day, just as we had in the beginning of our fall classes.

In early January we began studying how to predict a firm's need for money. Now, one month later, we were deep into efficient markets and diversification strategies. It was way over my head, but I struggled with each new concept, trying to fit it into what I already knew.

Our professor, Edward Stein, was having a rough go of it. There were a number of people in class who thought they knew a lot about finance and they openly argued with him whenever they got the chance. For his part, he would frustrate us by not really answering when we had legitimate questions. Instead, he would throw our questions back to the class and let students answer them. A lot of us thought he was a lousy professor, but my feelings weren't that strong. For me he made things as clear as I could handle them. Perhaps it was easier because I didn't know anything about finance before he walked in the door on the first day, so I had no Wall Street notions to discard.

The techniques we were learning were quite simple. The hard part was to put them all together and construct a useful financial theory. For example, the basic concept Edward tried to drive home was that return should equal risk. That is: return, the amount of money to be earned on an investment, should match risk, the uncertainty of getting the money. Therefore it followed that if I put equal amounts of money into a safe investment, say a bank savings account, and a riskier investment, say stock in Apple Computer, I could expect to earn more money from my investment in Apple because I took more risk. This is because the bank deposit is guaranteed by the government but I don't know if Apple Computer will be around in one, two, or ten years.

From this concept flowed case after case on measuring and diversifying risk. We learned that if risks can be estimated, then investments varying from U.S. government obligations, savings accounts, bonds, stocks, real estate, and oil and gas ventures to venture capital can be lined up with their appropriate riskiness. The amount of money that we expect to earn from each investment will correspond to our lineup. When we do this we can pick and choose among no-risk, moderate-risk, and very risky investments, so that we come out with an average rate of return. We learned that this strategy, called diversification, was the best way to protect against losing too much money on one investment. To me, it simply reduced itself to the maxim I learned from my grandmother: don't put all your eggs in one basket.

We learned other techniques: how to value a firm's assets and how to estimate the cost to a company if it sold stock or debt. Either the stock would have to pay the owner dividends or its price would have to increase in value in order to give its owner a return. If the company sold debts, usually bonds, the interest payment was the cost of the debt.

One month into these techniques we were asked to read a note on the "efficient markets hypothesis." I didn't understand it because it assumed that I knew and had absorbed most of the previous month's work. But Edward tried to explain it in class.

"Basically, all it says is that there are a lot of sharp analysts in Wall Street. Each one of them wants to make a buck for himself or for the company. He works long hours looking at companies and their products. He studies markets and predicts where the growth will be. Because each one works diligently and because there is so much competition among investment houses, all the information that is available to people who buy stocks is available at around the same time. If someone figures out that, say, IBM is ready to launch a new product that will probably be successful, he will buy the stock, knowing its value will rise. But information travels fast on Wall Street, therefore a lot of people will buy the stock. This will cause its price to go up, and thus the stock is not the bargain it was before. Stock markets, bond markets, and the money markets are efficient because all known information, both good and bad, is available to traders and thus reflected in prices."

It was an earful, and I wanted so much to understand it, but it came hard. So hard that I was lost in thought about efficient markets when Edward changed the discussion to the day's case. The case was COMSAT; we had to figure out how risky an investment in the Communications Satellite Corporation was. Either I looked totally confused or very knowledgeable, for Edward wrote a formula on the board, spun around, and headed right for me. He came up close, knocked on my desk three times and said, "What d'ya think, Fran?"

From out of the blue came my real self, indignant at his violation of my space, his rude knocking on my desk.

I knocked back three times and shouted, "I don't know."

I turned beet red. And so did Edward, though his shade of obvious embarrassment was more rose than beet. He posed his question differently and I stuttered out a reply, but he could tell that I needed help. Ron Watts raised his hand and answered it.

The whole class laughed at my "I don't know." I must have spoken for a lot of people because Alan Talmadge came up later, slapped me on the back, and said, "You said it for all of us."

And the next day Danielle showed me the *Skydeck News,*

which was a one-page newsletter written by those who occupied the top row of seats. In it they commented freely on the day's activities in Section D. On the bottom was "The Score for the Day": Edward 0; Fran 10.

Shortly afterward, I went to Edward's office and apologized, although it was clear to both of us I didn't have to. Out of frustration and fear I had responded in kind to his pressure on me, and there was something both scary and delightful about it. On the one hand, it was scary still to feel, in February, that I didn't know very much even though I loved Finance. On the other hand, it was delightful to know that I didn't care as much as I used to about learning every new concept and that somehow letting myself focus on what was really important would get me through first year without hitting the screen.

It wasn't confirmed that I would get through, but it was increasingly clear. I'd know for sure in late March, when we got our first set of final grades for OB, ME, and Control. The first inkling came as I sat down in January with Reva Cromwell, my Control tutor. For a solid, uninterrupted hour I asked her every question on my page-long list. She answered each one calmly and in no haste. It was the first time I had slowed down to learn since the Sunday before Thanksgiving when I studied for midterms.

Then, in early February, the night before our Managerial Economics final, Kate and I had dinner and a study session together. We shared our notes about regression analysis and linear programming. We recalled with a grin the look of dismay on the face of my old study group friend George Cohen when he had tried to give a few of us a review of linear programming a few days earlier.

"He was explaining log x and log y, do you remember, Kate?" I asked.

"And Devaki, bless her heart, raised her hand and said,

'What's log x mean?' He stopped talking then; he knew it was hopeless if we didn't even know logarithms. But, do you know, he had no idea what it was like not to understand what was such an obvious, basic concept."

"Yes, and we'll probably not understand it much tonight," I said as I began to pack up my books.

We'd studied for four hours and it was already 11 P.M. It was the only night I'd spent working so hard before an exam and I was tense about it.

"I'll walk you home and we can photocopy each other's notes in the Square, even though it's a futile gesture and we know it," I said.

It was a Friday night—very cold, perhaps zero or so, for the snow around was crusted and I felt numb even through my insulated gloves.

Kate said, "Sometimes when it's this cold I think of my grandmother out in Oklahoma at the turn of the century. They had to go out all the time at night in weather like this. It must have been very hard. And I think of my grandfather too. So strong and there for us, like a solid rock to get my toehold in."

As we walked I could feel our eyes fill. Even the cold couldn't prevent us from sharing the pain.

"I know what you're thinking, Kate. Probably if your grandparents were here they would say, 'Come now, sweetie, even if you don't do well, it'll be okay.'"

"Yes, they would say that," she said, and as I turned, I could see the frosted tears on her red cheeks.

"And for me, I must reach down again inside me and pull my insides out. Somehow it makes me stand up straighter."

"Fran, we'll probably fail."

"I know, Kate, but we've done the best we could."

Because the exam confirmed our worst expectations, we found it remarkably easy to laugh afterward. We both had the same response—how could four hours go by so slowly; we had nothing to say! One question, half the exam, was a regression analysis. It was a computer output showing baseball-game ticket sales, and the question concerned the effect on sales of hometown TV telecasts of the game. There were all kinds of variables to predict sales and we were supposed to analyze the output and write up a new program. Neither of us knew much about regression or about what made people go to baseball games, so we struck out on that one.

The other question was worse. It was on linear programming and asked which production critical path was better for building a ship. Again, we were given a computer output and asked to analyze and comment on it.

I said to myself and later to Kate, "It really doesn't matter. We can sail through HBS, never come close to the screen, and fail ME too. The only thing that matters is our bruised egos."

And by late February, the more I thought about it, the less it did matter. There were so many other things to keep us busy. The reading work load was so foolish that there wasn't a chance I could keep up. For three nights in a row we had more than one hundred twenty pages to read; that, plus getting ready for class the next day. We were deep into our Business, Government, and the International Economy course by then and had started another new course, Human Resources Management.

BGIE was pure fun. Since the goal of it was to introduce us to the relationship between government and business, I found it easy. The course was aimed at giving students a basis for understanding a country's strategy for industrialization and therefore would enable us to predict favorable economic conditions.

I also loved Dickson Grant, the professor. Although he was young and a recent honors graduate from the school, he possessed a self-assurance or worldliness that allowed his sensitivities to show. He was nervous in the classroom and sometimes aggressive, but he was very kind too, and when I visited him in his office, he said what no other professor had. "It's probably very hard for you at HBS, Fran, in that you're older and can't always see the value of what you have to contribute."

I agreed with him and told him how debilitating it was to feel stupid in the "numbers courses" when so many students so obviously understood.

"Try to keep in mind, Fran, that you know what you want out of this place. That's a real asset, since many people don't. They come here looking for a new direction, but it doesn't come easily. It takes a lot of soul searching."

"Dickson, you sound like you've been through it all. Have you?" I asked.

He answered after a few moments, no doubt wondering if he should be so personal. "In a way, yes. I worked for a consulting firm after graduating, but it wasn't right for me, so I'm here for a few years sorting out my future. The art of it is to know what *your* game is, not the game of the school. Of course, the school provides a fantastic education, and big businesses and consulting companies scoop up graduates right and left. But the companies want people in their mid-twenties who will do the hard work for them; for the most part they aren't looking for older students of your age. People like you are only a small fraction of the student body, so you don't get that much attention. And while it's easy to get caught up competing in their game—don't, because it'll make your life miserable."

"Do you mean getting honors, Dickson?"

"Yes, that, and other, more subtle things," he said.

"Like the one-up-manship that goes on and the feeling that everything I say in class is either totally ignored or laughed at or given a very small nod? I struggle with my ambivalence about competing with other students; sometimes I really want to and sometimes it makes me cringe."

"Just play your own game, Fran, and let everyone else play theirs. You can't compete at their game and that may cause you some pain, but remember, they can't compete at yours either."

With those words I left Dickson Grant's office, feeling very good. He offered to help me decide my next year's course work and I knew I'd visit him again soon to discuss it. And I was ready to start thinking about next year's work, assuming as I looked at the course catalog that I would be at school. Since the first-year curriculum was required, it was exciting to think about second year because only one course was required and we had free rein over the rest of our schedule.

By the end of February, our first-year course work changed too. The critical skill was no longer number crunching and interpreting, but rather assimilating large amounts of material. This was more doable for humanities-trained students. While the daily grind of reading and analyzing cases did not change, there was somehow a different kind of pressure in class. The most obvious change was the freedom from MC, Control, and OB. Because those finals were earlier in the month, there was room in our schedule for the new courses—Human Resources Management and a course that would begin in a few weeks, Business Policy. My current courses, BGIE, Finance, MC, and HRM were easy to relate to and, except for Finance, didn't require mastery of new, totally unfamiliar techniques in order to do each day's cases.

By now school had become almost enjoyable. Human Resources Management was a case in point. HRM was designed to give us the skills needed to manage employees, be they professional, blue collar, or white collar. It was also a course that helped students design coherent people strategies so that companies' product and market strategies meshed with their human relations policies. In a nitty-gritty way, the course taught us how to negotiate with labor unions and to foresee, instead of react to, employee grievances.

One of the first assignments in HRM was to read a technical note on the coal industry and watch the film *Harlan County*. *Harlan County* is a documentary film about the struggles of coal miners to bring a union into a company that produces coal in a small Kentucky town. It is a ruthlessly honest view of organizing activities of the miners and their families. As such, it was our first look, while at Harvard, into the lives and feelings of workers. And it was a powerful experience. Sitting in the auditorium, I could feel the agony of the students as we watched the miners get together and confront management, the Peabody Coal Company.

The next day before class began, I heard some commotion outside the class door. Students were organizing! They objected to a group MC assignment we were required to do over our coming weekend break. Michael Mitchell, Ron Watts, and Ramon Pires were distributing song sheets. We were going to start HRM class with a protest song against the school and its policies. When the professor walked in, so did Ramon, Ron, and Michael, dressed in overalls and wearing hats. They held signs that said PICKET and STRIKE. And they led us in song. On cue, we sang all four verses of the song they had composed before class and then picked up our name cards and set them vertically into the notches in front of us. About half the class joined the protest.

Our professor, Roger Winchester, wore a patient but pained expression on his face. I looked at him closely. He was a very fine person, and he had a rich history of labor union and employee-related work experience. The class of 1982 was the first class to take Human Resources Management, as it was newly introduced this year in recognition of the difficulties American managers were having with their work forces. Roger Winchester was instrumental in designing and administering the course, but none of his planning had prepared him to watch HBS students, future managers, identify with the coal miners' unions and organize against the school.

Our action did eventually lead to some changes in the MC calendar, but by the middle of the same HRM class, we had all moved our name cards to their proper position. We were students again, the protest over. And then we began talking about the real-life problems of workers. Danielle raised her hand and Roger asked her what she thought.

Her eyes were troubled and she spoke softly: "I think we all have to remember, as we sit in our big offices with our fat promotions, that we are comfortable. Most of all, safe. The work in the coal mines is life or death for these people and that's something we'll never face."

Danielle meant what she said. She looked like she was close to tears, but she didn't say anything more.

Roger turned to the class and said, "Yes, I know."

But he didn't add anything to what Danielle had said and didn't continue the discussion, instead recognizing another student and moving to another point. As I sat there I felt—what?—a curious sense of the moment. Here we all were, able and ready to talk about workers, their lives, their priorities. We were ready, through the film and through Danielle's comment, to investigate what "human" meant in the Human Resources Management course. But we couldn't do it. We couldn't put "them" on an equal footing with "us." It was as if understanding what it was all about for a worker might weaken us, cause us pain, make us question. And even though the course was designed for us to grapple with some of these concepts, we had gotten just a shade too close to the heat of a fire and we had backed away fast.

I found myself thinking of the HRM class long after it was over. How I loved Danielle for bringing up that point! At that moment I realized how important it was for women to be in our section in at least the numbers we were. As women we didn't change the system; most of us didn't seem to want to. But what we did do was push for and allow a little more gentle, human understanding to come through all of the tough stuff we learned day in, day out. It was the same old thing I knew from my work in the women's movement. Women allow themselves to cry. It's a strength, not a weakness, as it is so often viewed. The tears that show pain also release it and allow a quiet, firm strength to be nurtured and to grow.

This facility doesn't come from our sexual difference from men. It seems to come from the social difference, the training that lets us cry from infancy onward. Of course, it's the opposite for men. They shield their emotions with bravado. As soon as boys are old enough, they are shamed out of crying when they hurt. These thoughts raced through my head as I thought about Danielle's comment and Roger's moving on to another subject. The class had eagerly followed his new train of thought. Why hadn't I said something? It would have been a perfect time to talk about how I felt about workers and the necessity of listening, really listening, to what they had to say.

There were times before today when I could have spoken from a more political point of view. But I didn't speak because no one would have heard. It was impossible to move the class into an area, or have them listen to something, that was outside the professor's scope for class discussions. And I could always sense that scope from the kinds of questions professors asked.

My mind kept moving along, connecting my thoughts and setting off a chain reaction that was outside my conscious control. I thought again of the women in the class and how the men sometimes just assumed their needs took precedence over ours. I thought of Stan Hooper and the end of BGIE class the day before. Robert McNamara, retired president of the World Bank, had been in class to discuss with us the need for industrialized countries to promote the development of nonindustrialized countries. It was an exciting class and it ended too soon. Kate and I were leaning over our desks, heads together, while students got up to leave.

"Do you remember Robert McNamara, Fran, and how we felt about him?" Kate asked.

"I do; right in the middle of the Vietnam War he was the only person in Washington we talked about," I said.

"McNamara symbolized the worst," Kate said, "the evil we were doing in Vietnam, murdering children, napalm—the war machine. Today he seemed to be atoning. The man who ordered villages eradicated is worrying about how to feed the poor of the world."

Crash! Crash! All of a sudden Stan Hooper banged my name card down on the desk in the six inches between Kate's face and mine. Our heads jerked back and we looked up at him, our conversation halted in midsentence. I couldn't think of anything to say, but Kate was steaming mad. She spit out, "What's the matter Stan, do you need a little attention?"

He grinned and said, not at all sheepishly, "Well, what d'ya think?"

Kate was still mad. I could tell by her white knuckles and by the way she said, "I think it's time to go."

Stan didn't have a clue what was wrong and he probably didn't care. But as Kate and I walked through the campus and over the bridge, we talked more about how little room there was for the womanly, sensitive sides of ourselves. I told her a story I had mentioned to no one, even though it had bothered me for the past few days.

"Ron Watts was standing in the hall with a couple of the men from our section the other day. I walked by and do you know what he said? 'What Ms. Margaret MC needs is a good fuck!' "

"Oh, come on," Kate said. "That stuff is from the last decade."

"I wish I were kidding. I was embarrassed for her because you know how those guys hang around her office being nice, trying to get a decent grade."

"Why do they think that women who speak back to them need sex, especially their sex?" Kate said. "What a joke."

"Well, MC is the only class where the professor gives regular grades. We get graded on our speeches, graded on our papers, and graded on our group assignments. We know every week where we stand. Maybe it's too much pressure for them not knowing in any other course where they stand, so the one person they hear feedback from, conveniently a woman, they trash."

"That's a pretty farfetched theory, Fran," Kate said with a smile. "But it wouldn't surprise me if it bugs them that she's in a position superior to them. Somehow they bring her down by saying she needs a good fuck. And that gives me the willies because I've been elected to be a president for the Business Game. That means I'll have to deal with the same thing."

"You'll do very well, Kate, and I can't wait," I said with glee. "I wish I were on your team."

"In the meantime I've got a story for you," Kate said. "You know, people are beginning to think about interviewing for summer jobs. Well, Carol Mathias is going out with a man in Section F. She said they worked out a strategy for interviewing to let them spend the summer together. First he would find a job in one of three cities they wanted to live in.

Then, when he had said yes, she'd follow and work there too."

"Boy, not hard to tell whose job comes first there, is it?"

We talked more about interviewing. There had been a big change in our class in the past few weeks and I was curious about it. Since I planned to work in my own business during the coming summer, I was not at all involved in what now was a daily routine of dressing up and meeting with recruiters.

At Harvard, interviewing for jobs was taken very seriously. There was an office dedicated to the process, called the Office for Career Development, and a separate library, called the Cole Room, which housed all of the career information. Hundreds of recruiters came to campus from January to March. Aptly called recruiting season, this time was important for first years because during the summer they had a chance to try out an industry or job that interested them. It was an important time for second years because they negotiated and decided on their favorite industry and company.

The recruiting process was formalized. Only recruiters who registered with the Office for Career Development and who followed HBS rules could recruit HBS students on campus. The rules included a ban on recruiting at other than prescribed times and a pledge not to employ any high pressure tactics to get students to commit to a particular firm. Students usually picked a dozen or so companies to interview with. They wrote letters to the companies of their choice, and if invited to interview, they were assigned half-hour slots in the recruiter's schedule. The recruiters and students met in the study group carrels in Aldrich Hall.

At first in class in mid-February I noticed only that the men were getting haircuts. Then the beards and moustaches were gone. By the end of the month, men and women were wearing suits and bringing briefcases to class. First-year students were not supposed to interview during class time, but that was a hard rule to enforce since we were in class almost all day. There were dinner parties, cocktail receptions, and Saturday interviews for three solid weeks. Some of the students who interviewed at three or four places were bleary-eyed in the mornings from the additional pressure of selling themselves while drinking bottles of wine and then doing cases at night.

Getting good jobs, getting the best offer they could, was the whole point of going to the school for many students. The MBA gave them an entree into a world of their choice. The range in summer salaries for Harvard MBAs in 1981 was $1,350 to $3,600 a month. Many of the students who got these offers had only a few years' experience in a working environment before coming to school, but students from Harvard were aggressively recruited because employers believed they had an education no other training program could beat.

Kate was under a lot of pressure to get the right job, and I could feel the tension under the surface of her smile as she talked. She wanted a job in the financial area, and it was hard for her to get recruiters to listen when they looked at her liberal arts background and political work experience. Southern real estate development and investment banking companies were recruiting on campus, but they were renowned for their lack of interest in women students. One company, which Kate would have loved to work for when she graduated, had never hired a woman MBA. She wondered aloud if she could be the first.

"You'd think, wouldn't you, that having gotten through this program, our femaleness wouldn't be an issue," she said half to herself, half to me.

"Didn't you hear what Sheryl Shaw said at WSA the other

day?" I replied. "She overheard two French students talking. They actually said that it's the craze in France now for men to marry a woman MBA or M.D., then to have her stay home and take care of children. It's a status symbol."

I continued, "But you know and I know that we're not going through all this to be anyone's status symbol. I won't even be anyone's token. Those times have passed."

"We hope," Kate said, mindful of Houston. "It's still the good old boys down there, you know. And I wonder how I'll fit in when I go home and mix with my husband's clients and their wives and all the social stuff that comes with doing business in the South."

"I wish we could will away the threatening feelings people get when women assert themselves. Just think about Sarah Ann. She wants to move to Atlanta with Jack when she graduates. It's a city with a lot of new growth and change, but I bet it's as tough as nails to get in that inner circle if you're female."

"I think it's tough as nails to just get your foot in the door unless you work for a national company or are literally a golden-haired whiz kid," Kate said.

For some time we walked along lost in our own thoughts. Now I could see the competition in class really assert itself. Those consulting firms rumored to be the best: McKinsey, Boston Consulting Group, and Booz-Allen, wouldn't give a second interview to students who expected any Low Passes. Investment banking houses like Goldman, Sachs and Salomon Brothers wanted finance "jocks" and routinely asked students at what age they'd begun investing in the stock market. Even if these weren't the careers or companies students wanted before they came to school, it appeared to me as though they were sucked into them by the pressure of wanting what everyone else wanted.

I felt the pressure too. It came as a surprise because it was so unexpected. Since I'd made my plans and was happy with them, I was relieved at not having to write letters, dress up, and go from class to an interview in no time flat. But after a few weeks of watching people come and go in their interview clothes, I found myself dressing better, shedding my jeans for a skirt, and wearing a coat instead of my warm down jacket.

At one point I even became defensive about my business as more than one student asked what I was doing for the summer. When I answered that I'd work for one or two clients we had, they asked how it could interest me to do something I'd done before coming to school.

It was very hard for me to explain. I'd already earned a big office, a nice title, and a fat salary working for someone else. It was interesting, but it just didn't excite me anymore. My business gave me the freedom to work with whom I pleased. But most of my colleagues were in their mid-twenties, and when I was their age I had felt as they did, so I tried not to take their questions too harshly.

During recruiting season it was fascinating to explore the priorities my classmates had when looking for summer jobs. Money and permanent job potential were at the top of the list. Geography didn't seem very important to a lot of students. I found this out in a conversation with Ron Watts one day when we talked about our futures. He asked me where I planned to settle.

When I told him western Massachusetts, he warned me, "But Massachusetts has one of the highest tax rates in the country."

Frankly, it had never occurred to me to care about the tax rate. "But what difference does the tax rate make—western Massachusetts and the Berkshire Mountains is some of the prettiest country I've ever seen."

"Pretty is not the issue. How much you have to pay is. I'm heading for the South."

We sat across from one another, Ron and I, pushing a little to find out why on earth the other could feel that way. I couldn't imagine spending my best years in an environment I didn't care for, and he couldn't imagine caring about anything but the economics of the decision that faced him.

It wasn't too long before the interview process was over. Most students found jobs, but some didn't and it worried them, as though they were somehow less capable because they hadn't gotten offers as quickly. There was a lot of measuring up in class; rumors spread quickly about who was offered what job. George Cohen decided to work with a consulting company, as did Sheryl Shaw, Michael Mitchell, and Susan Mantero. Sarah Ann planned to work for a computer software company in Massachusetts. Kate was still looking for a position with one of the biggest real estate developers in Houston, but she expected to work at getting the job long after recruiting season was over. This was typical for students who didn't get jobs with the big companies in February.

By the end of February, everyone was ready for our vacation, a five day spring break. The last two days in February, we had our Finance and BGIE midterm exams. When we came back to school after vacation, we would participate in a week-long Business Game.

I wasn't sure how I felt about the game. It wasn't graded and students weren't compelled to participate. It was almost the only event of our first year about which we had a choice. The game was a computer-simulated competition between companies. There were seven companies carved out of Section D; Kate had been elected to head one of them. And each of us had been assigned to one of the companies to help it win.

The firms all competed in manufacturing and selling a product in domestic and overseas markets. The product was a SHIRE, a mythical object that was a cross between a shirt and a tire. The president of a company gathered his or her team together and assigned jobs to the strongest people. There were vice-presidents for production, marketing, and finance. Other team members did "grunt work," which usually meant analysis and number crunching. When we were given our SHIRE materials, we had a stack of raw data six inches high, so there was a lot of analysis to do: figuring out seasonal demand, projected sales in various regions of the world, material shortages and lead times, and the cost of financing planned strategies. It was quite an undertaking.

I was fascinated when Kate ran for company president. She didn't like competition any more than I did, but she saw it as a challenge and thought if she were president she'd take it seriously and learn more. Before the break, she told me her goal for the team was to keep all twelve members involved in the game all week. Kate's goal was not the same as nearly everyone else's—winning. I knew she'd learn a lot; the game gave us our first opportunity to synthesize our course work and look at business decisions as a whole unit, from the top and strategically. I respected her resolve to join in the competition but was wary of it for me. I left for the week's vacation, my first hassle-free week off since coming to school, and decided to think about the game when I returned.

Seven days later, I was almost my old self again. During the week off I had called friends spontaneously, without the weight of cases hanging over my head. In the morning I'd filled my coffee cup two or three times, savoring the precious choice of what to do with my day. I couldn't give my life back over to Harvard so easily, I found when Sunday night rolled around and my company was scheduled to meet at 7 P.M. in the Pub; I didn't go.

My company's president, Richard Travis, wasn't in the next evening when I called to tell him I wasn't going to participate in the game. It didn't seem to matter much to him, since he didn't return my call. I assumed he had his executives lined up and working and I wasn't one of the buddies he could depend upon.

I caught myself feeling guilty for my decision later that day. I was caught between what I needed and wanted. I needed a week to work with Joyce on our business, but I wanted to feel that I'd worked hard enough at school. Not participating in the Business Game would cause the familiar tug I felt each night when I put down my pencil and turned the lights off. Had I done enough? Had I tried hard enough to understand?

Struggling to accept myself and my sense of inadequacy was an endless chore. I was so hard on myself, expecting to have energy to do more each time I crawled up a mountain and reached a plateau. When I should have been resting and enjoying my success, I busied myself by focusing on the next challenge. Now, at thirty-three, I had an intellectual understanding of this phenomenon: by keeping busy I didn't feel the exhaustion or the pain of the moment. I could fool the gullible part of myself into believing that I'd be pleased with my accomplishments after the next obstacle was overcome.

A watchful sixth sense took over during the week of the Business Game. I had to pull away from school and gather in my reserve strength to push through to the end of the year. I didn't step foot on campus all week. Instead, Joyce and I worked together for the next few days and produced the much needed copy for our business brochure, without which we couldn't market. We mapped out our work schedule for the summer, too—a schedule that allowed me plenty of time to rest before school began again in September.

Kate called the following Saturday night. It was March 14 and the game was over. I had tried to call her two or three times during the week, but she hadn't been home, and I had assumed she was immersed in moves and counter moves. She sounded worn thin, and I knew she must have worked very hard. She asked Joyce and me to meet her at Regina's for a pizza.

We were late, but when we joined Kate we realized she didn't notice us because her eyes were glazed over with exhilaration and Chianti.

"Champ. How did it go? We thought about you all week," I said with a grin.

"Hey, I can't exactly tell you what business strategies we used," Kate said, "but I can tell you two things I did learn: you gotta go after your competition 'balls out,' and when you lose, you gotta learn how to 'take it in the shorts.'"

We were in hysterics. We shared our crazy visions of Kate leading the troops into battle balls out and wondered if women would ever need an equivalent expression. What would it be? Boobs out? Buns out? We strained to understand what use it would be to go after competition balls out. And to take it in the shorts. From what we knew about men's shorts, we could imagine it hurt like hell to take it in the shorts. Did we have to grapple with these things in order to be great general managers? Kate thought so.

"Listen, our language doesn't have any meaning to them. It was hard enough to direct this group without trying to impose my interpretation of power on them."

"Tell us about the game and how you did it," Joyce said. "Who won? Did you have a good time?"

"Well, I'm exhausted, but it was worth it. Our company didn't place badly at all. We came out third from the top. The measures, you know, were profitability and market share. At the end, the group that won had only four out of the original twelve people left playing on the team. The president of that team didn't even participate in the last few days."

"Which team was it and why not?" I asked.

"Company Two won," Kate replied. "They won because the only measure of winning was how much money they made and to do it they pared down to the four smartest people. Stan Hooper and Michael Mitchell were in the final four, and so were Susan Mantero and Ramon Pires. They wouldn't have anything to do with Rudolf Ziegler, the president of their company, because they thought he wasn't aggressive enough. And they worked their tails off, day and night. Every time one of my people went to the computer room, one of the four was there doing computer simulations on a planned strategy. They had us beaten hands down because they were so focused and because they worked so hard."

I hadn't been assigned to Company Two, but Kate's retelling of her stories made me glad I hadn't participated at all. It was no fun to compete for what seemed to me no good reason at all.

"How did your team do?"

"We hung in there," Kate said proudly. "Every one of the twelve assigned to Company Six was working at the end of the week. And I think we all had a good time, even though we didn't win. Some of the men were frustrated with me because I didn't give enough strategic direction, but I warned them at the beginning of the week that I didn't see that as my role. Besides, reading mountains of computer output was no easier for me than it was on the Managerial Economics final. My role was to hold us all together."

Oh, she looked so proud. It felt good to sit in Regina's with a glass of Chianti and look at my friend Kate, the same friend who, afraid to fail with me, had quivered in the cold one month ago. She had more to tell us, and we listened eagerly.

"I can't put it together yet," she said. "It seems like a strange set of priorities to me, to only value the economic outcome of the business game and nothing else. It makes a joke of our classes in Organizational Behavior and Human Resources Management. More clearly than anything else we've read or heard, it made me understand what Harvard is all about—making money."

"How crass," Joyce and I said in unison. But then we'd discussed Harvard in those terms many times before. Making money was important, knowing how to make money was even more important, but neither one was the be-all and end-all of our lives. This one-dimensional focus of the program made me question my presence in the school more often than I let on. It suddenly hit me that I hadn't wanted any part of the competition of the Business Game because I hadn't wanted to deal with having profitability and market share as the only measures of my team's success. I respected Kate even more for her participation.

"It's not that we didn't compete," Kate continued. "In fact I found myself pushing the men on my team to be as aggressive as they could be. We had midnight trips to other companies' trash cans to dig out the computer output on their costs and inventory levels. And we nosed around overhearing conversations whenever we could. It's just that on the whole it meant more to have everyone making decisions and working together than to increase third-quarter profitability."

We were three glasses of wine into the evening by now and getting more philosophical by the minute.

Joyce spoke up. "It's impressive to listen to you, Kate. I've wondered since September if one of you would begin to change, to become so money centered that you lost the sensitivity that made you both special in my eyes. But you haven't, and hearing you tonight, I'm convinced that even if Harvard has broken you into pieces, it hasn't remade you in its image."

Our eyes were glistening as we unsteadily got up to leave.

"Ah, yes, we're proud too," Kate said as she looked at me. "The sad thing is that in Finance we're learning what it's really all about, and one thing I do understand between our efficient markets and capital asset pricing models is that being sensitive won't sell on Wall Street. Cold hard cash and maximizing shareholder value is what the markets are all about."

We decided to tackle that problem another time. Right now Kate and I were content to have the spirit of our old selves intact. Both of us went home knowing that we would get through Harvard in spite of everything.

By mid-March the grind of cases picked up some speed, and there were many changes in Section D. With the new courses, and all of the beards and longish hair gone, it was not the same old place. People didn't wear flannel shirts and jeans anymore. More women wore skirts and tailored blouses even though interviewing was over. We now had Business Policy, a course that taught us business planning and corporate strategy, and we picked up Marketing again.

Even the old fear about Marketing was gone. Thomas Rhinehart looked like the same person we had faced last November, but his stature and control of the class were gone. It was as though all of us were building our egos, bit by bit, and we didn't need to clog up the process by worrying about what Thomas thought about us. I went to see him one day before Marketing class began; it was the recommended procedure if a student had gotten a Low Pass on an exam. As in the fall, students were scheduled back to back, so we only had fifteen minutes to tell him our strategy for getting a Sat. Thomas hardly remembered my exam or my Low Pass, which, the more I thought about it, was a relief.

As I sat in front of him, I realized I didn't have to do much to get a Sat, because only eight of our eighty-five would get a Low Pass at the end of the term and I talked too much in class to deserve such a fate. Why couldn't I have had that perspective in December and saved myself tears and heartache? Instead of answering my own question, I found myself saying, "Thomas, I plan to hand in a written report. Which case do you recommend?"

"Daisy Razor, Poland Water, or BIC Pens are all good cases," he replied.

I dutifully wrote his suggestions down. The thought of writing out a case analysis for Marketing chilled me to the bone as I immediately recalled my disaster of a midterm. But the other alternative was to request that Thomas call on me to open a case, and I didn't want to put myself in such a position. Talking in class wasn't that easy.

"How's the class going?" Thomas asked. "Who are the frequent talkers now?"

"Class is almost boring," I replied. "We're tired of each other's bullshit, and saying things just to score points is no fun for anyone."

I couldn't believe I was being so honest with him. Why was I telling him what I really thought? Because it was a struggle not to, because there were so few occasions and there was little reason to connect, one human with another.

But I didn't have much time to talk; his schedule was backed up, and Ron Watts and Tony Giambelli were waiting right outside his door. Ron, Tony, and I exchanged sheepish looks: so you got a Low Pass too, was what we all thought.

Kate and Sarah Ann walked by as I headed out his door,

and I shared my discomfort at being in Rhinehart's office. Kate broke into a big smile.

"That's nothing—you'll never guess what I dreamed last night. I was jogging along the Charles River and whom should I see but Thomas. He gave me a big hello and I stopped. Instead of shaking his hand or greeting him, I found myself in a rage. I picked him up by his red plaid tie and backed him up to the nearest tree, whereupon I smacked him across the face, whap, whap, whap. And let him go, saying, 'Now you know what I feel like in your class, Thomas.'"

"Lord," said Sarah Ann. "That's not a dream for the weakhearted. Please try to contain yourself for tomorrow's class or you'll bite his head off!"

"I'm all right now," she replied. "My dream released all the rage I had. Now I'm ready for two more months of Thomas Rhinehart and Marketing. It's not the biggest thing that will happen tomorrow, anyway, since I just saw Rick Cabot and he said that tomorrow the registrar is handing out final grades in OB, ME, and Control."

Tomorrow was March 20: it would be the first time since registration in September that we would know definitively where we stood compared to our section mates. Sarah Ann looked patient with us; she knew she'd get a decent grade in ME and probably Control, although she wasn't as sure about OB. We were much more vulnerable.

OB was the only grade we were sure about. We could feel each other going over the litany in our heads again for the umpteenth time: a loop in ME and maybe one in Control, that means four credits of loops because each course is worth two credits; if we loop two credits in Finance, POM, or Marketing, that means we have to pass MC, HRM, and Business Policy because they're each worth one credit and two of those loops would equal eight credits of loop, the magic number at which we hit the screen.

Loops used to be so innocent. They were just the circles in the vacuum cleaner hose or in a knotted necklace. For the few minutes we three stood together and compared our anxieties, loops were everything.

"Well, we'll know tomorrow—three cases away," I said.

And so we found ourselves a day later on the lawn in front of the library—Baker Beach, as it is affectionately called. It was a foggy day, the kind that Boston strings out for seven weeks and calls spring. It was too damp for a down jacket but too cold for my raincoat. I stood shivering with Kate and Sarah Ann as we held our unopened envelopes out in front of us. Rick Cabot had handed them out as soon as Marketing had ended, a few minutes before. We moved out of the room in a unit, not looking to one side or the other. I heard Pat Worth and Stan Hooper in the hall; they were excited, apparently they had gotten two E's each.

As we opened our envelopes, I started to move toward the street. I could feel my anxiety creeping up and knew I would want to run if my grades were bad. I didn't want anything to do with the campus, and my courage to face the moment was leached away by months of worry and pent-up insecurity.

"How'd ya do, champ?" I asked boldly.

We were looking at our grades at the same time, taking in the verdicts with a gulp.

"Two Sats and a loop," Kate said.

"Three Sats," Sarah Ann said.

"One Sat, one loop, and an E," I said.

"We'll make it, we'll make it, we made it," Kate said. "Yeah!"

Kate and I looked at each other with gratitude.

We had both gotten a Sat in Control. Kirk Cranston had given us a Sat in Control. Thank God.

And we had both looped ME; how could we have avoided it with that computer crap and critical fractile stuff we'd never heard of before?

"And, Sarah Ann, we're proud of you, all Sats," Kate said, beaming from head to toe.

"An E among us, now that's something to be proud of," Sara Ann said.

"Oh, it's just OB," I said. "I didn't work hard in OB at all, and no matter how happy I am about Control, I can't help but resent that loop in ME. Why didn't we get ME?"

"Think of it this way," Sarah Ann said. "In Business Policy we're learning about business strategy and concentrating in market niches. Well you both did the same thing—concentrating in Control—you did what you had to do to get through."

"Yeah, we took a loop, the strategic loop," Kate said.

They had a point, and from that moment that's just the way I thought about it: my very own strategic loop.

6

TOUGHING IT OUT

It is Monday, April 6, and the first day of Production and Operations Management for the spring. We're a different section from the one Duke Moore left in December. Not all of us are prepared for every class, and we make fun of cases more openly than we would have dared last semester.

Duke strolled into class with a big smile on his face, full of encouragement and enthusiasm. He looked like a different person too—all of his previous capacity to frighten has vanished.

"Well, hello, it's good to see you," he said to the class. "Is Fran Henry here?"

I raised my hand. He had trouble finding me because since our last POM class I had moved from the left side of the room to the right so I could sit with Kate and Sarah Ann. When he spotted me, he asked if I would open the day's case: New Balance Athletic Shoes USA. I wasn't as jolted as before and even found myself pleased because Duke knew that as a runner I would understand the case.

I hadn't been called on to open a case since the first week in September. I worried about opening in Marketing and Managerial Economics, but I hadn't been called on and when professors asked for volunteers to open, as they occasionally did, I never raised my hand. But my sixth sense told me I would be called on in POM, especially because of the warning Duke had given me on my midterm, the message that told me I was "too close to a Low Pass for comfort." The night before, I had come back to Cambridge from a weekend with clients in Washington and was tired at seven o'clock when I got to my apartment and pulled out my cases. Something had told me to do POM carefully, however, when I looked at the assignment.

New Balance Athletic Shoes USA was a case that presented the problem of factory expansion. Should New Balance move out of its crowded Massachusetts facilities and build in Ireland, New Hampshire, or Texas? In addition to analyzing the case, we were asked to read an article entitled "Plant Location Decisions." As I sat reading it and reviewing New Balance's options, I recalled the POM case that Kate had opened in the fall. It was the only case on non-profits assigned, and since Kate's background was in the arts, she had known Duke was being supportive when he called on her to open it.

I was in Kate's league when it came to relating to non-profits rather than factories and industrial products. And since I was a jogger, I reasoned Duke might be tempted to call on me to open New Balance. My expectations were fulfilled, and as I raised my hand, I began to get my thoughts in order.

"New Hampshire is my choice for expanding," I said. "I

looked at the labor pool available, the shipping and inventory carrying costs, the capacity to make shoes for each projected factory, the tax rate, and local economic incentives. I reviewed each of these criteria, keeping in mind the kind of product New Balance is manufacturing—high quality running shoes."

With that beginning, I presented each option and talked for five or so minutes about New Balance and its reputation for manufacturing running shoes.

Duke wrote most of what I said on the blackboard, and when I finished, he turned and said, "What about the economics of the options? Did you look at that?"

I had, and offered the income statement I had drawn up for the New Hampshire facility. I hadn't projected income for more than two years.

"Did you do an income statement for more than the first years or for the Ireland or Texas option?" Duke asked.

"No I didn't; I just wanted to make sure a New Hampshire plant wasn't a wash, because I chose it on other grounds."

At that point Duke turned to the class and opened the discussion for comment. A flurry of hands went up and I listened as each option was reviewed again. I tried to appear self-confident, but it was hard because I knew a major weakness had been exposed; I hadn't done the economics of each choice. The economics of a business decision was almost everything in courses like ME and Finance. In POM it was much more important than I had demonstrated with my single income statement. What I should have done was project sales for each location and do an income statement for a few years at least. When would I catch up and feel as though I'd done a really good job, even an adequate one?

Cases and case discussion were beginning to drag me down. At first, especially in the fall, it had been exciting to pick through forty pages of detail and distill some new, useful information from each case. Because we had done three cases each and every night for the past eight months, by April we had been exposed to virtually every type of company and industry: computer hardware, airplanes, retailing, wholesaling, consumer goods manufacture, steel and coal, and on and on. Sometimes company names were disguised, but often not, so we became familiar with the problems of Bethlehem Steel, General Motors, and TRW. When I read the *Wall Street Journal* or listened to the news, it was easy to understand the context of a story line and thus it seemed the little bits of case information added up to a well-rounded view of big business life in the United States.

But by spring my mind was like a fuzzball. It was becoming hard to keep the information straight, and it was frustrating to whiz through a case, perhaps never to read about the company again. We solved its problems in two hours of reading and eighty minutes of class discussion and that was that. There was no time in our schedule for thoughtful reappraisal. This was not true for all students. Some people understood the material well enough to spend thirty minutes each night listing the main points from the day's discussions. Kirk Cranston, my Control instructor, had suggested this method to the class in the fall, telling us that if we invested time in reflecting on what we'd learned it would be easier to review for exams.

And, I thought to myself, if I had a computer brain like Kirk and had been a CPA before coming to Harvard, I would have done it too. Instead, each afternoon when I sat down to work on the next day's cases it was all I could do to put the old cases away. It was painful to try and review them because everything I didn't understand from the day's discussion would be thrown back in my face again and if I started I knew I would never settle down and get the next day's work done.

I wasn't just tired of doing cases, I was tired of the case content too. For one thing some were written poorly, and for another too many were still sexist. I knew the Women's Student Association mounted a heroic effort to get the generic "he" out of cases. They had succeeded and cases were much better than even five years ago, when Holly Winthrop was in school and women were never mentioned in class or cases except as consumers.

But the case content and substance hadn't changed that much, and I was weary of the way male business executives viewed women. In Business Policy just a few weeks ago, for example, our first case and class was Head Ski, and the case quoted Mr. Head commenting on the behavior of the purchasers of ski equipment. Men buy the equipment for skiing; "girls" buy it for the lodge activities. And when I started to think about cases, I remembered L'eggs in Marketing and how uncomfortable it made me to hear my colleagues discuss women's pantyhose habits.

And the case we did that very week in Marketing caused my unease to boil into a rage. The case, Daisy, was about the women's shaving market and asked us to design a marketing strategy for a new safety razor by Gillette. The case was reasonably straightforward; it presented information about the competition, Flicker, and didn't get into much detail about consumers of the product. When Thomas ended class I was glad to have the case behind me, so I was shocked when he announced that the day's case was in fact called Daisy A and that we'd do a series on Daisy for the next week and a half. The series also included Daisy B, C, D, and E. Each of these would delve into another aspect of marketing strategy: the competition, product positioning, advertising, test marketing, and implementation.

I was sick to my stomach by page 3 of Daisy B. Here I found everything I couldn't stand about business and society's pressure contained in a comment by the Gillette executive who managed the introductory campaign for Daisy:

> From the fifty-seven women interviewed, Alison Yancy learned that, while women tended to perceive shaving products and the act of shaving as masculine, they considered the end results to be feminine. Most said that shaving made them feel cleaner and more feminine, but they did not view it as a glamorous or pleasant task. Most considered it as a necessary evil, comparable to eyebrow plucking. They felt that the dictates of modern American society were such that, in order for a woman to be considered well groomed, feminine, and appealing to men, her skin should be smooth and almost totally void of hairy stubble. Thus, they said, young girls were conditioned at an early age via romantic stories, mass consumer advertising campaigns, and peer groups to believe that removing hair, particularly from the legs, was necessary for social acceptance. . . . The women surveyed felt that shaving did not add to their appearance in a positive sense, but that it prevented potential "detraction" from their appearance by removing unsightly hair.

It was hard to read and not want to tear it up. I was angry for all of the unfair advertising I remembered, aimed at keeping healthy women young, skinny, smoking, and drinking. Yet advertisers argued that they simply reflected what consumers already desired. It seemed like a rationalization for a multitude of sins, sins against women, since so much of print and TV advertising was directed at the woman purchaser.

There was nothing to be done about it at Harvard, though,

for I had learned already that the strength of my emotion about a particular issue had absolutely no bearing on whether anyone in class listened to me or agreed with my point of view. The comments people were most likely to listen to were either funny or very powerful "rational" arguments.

I developed a fantasy about having a marketing case on some male personal product, like Cruex, for jock itch. Now *that,* I thought, would give all the women in the class the opportunity to sit back and watch the men squirm as we discussed consumer preferences for this type of scent or that type of spray. My fantasy never came to life. We never once discussed a personal product for men in any of our classes.

Another aspect of cases bothered me: the fact that women were so rarely portrayed as principal characters in cases. As future women executives, it was tiring to discuss case after case with "Mr. Davis" making all the decisions. I found myself asking a number of professors and people in WSA why there weren't more cases about women's adventures in corporate decision making.

The usual response was predictable: there aren't enough female top executives from whom to get cases. One conversation stopped me dead in my tracks. It was with Mary Smythe, a first-year student and WSA member, who wanted to change the way women were viewed at the school. She had pursued the subject with the head of case research, a man in his middle years. He had said he was committed to doing something about it, but there just weren't enough women executives. She went further, asking him why he didn't just change some men's names to women's. He surprised her and said he had tried but that it hadn't worked. Each person or company that is the subject of a case has the right to read and approve or disapprove it, and the fellow he had suggested it to had balked. He had asked the executive what the problem was. His response: was my performance in the case so bad that you want to make me a woman?

Oh my God; oh my God. The collective ego of WSA must have been crushed by that one. It was exhausting to think about these things and try to do cases at the same time. It was enough just to get the work done and not fall prey to the hype that I might flunk out without trying to change too much about the way Harvard operated. Thus, my conversation with Mary Smythe made me respect WSA even more. But once I had started to muse about Harvard from a woman's perspective, other aspects of my education began to demand attention. One was the labels we put on concepts we learned.

Finance terms were my favorites, particularly the ones I learned from a second-year student. As we sat one day analyzing a merger, she said that it was just the old "seduce and abandon" strategy.

"Seduce and abandon?" I said, wondering how on earth this expression had found its way into Finance.

"Yes, that's the strategy when a firm wants to take over another and woos it with promises of all it will do when it becomes parent. Then, once the merger has taken place, the acquired company finds itself out on a limb ready for liquidation. Haven't you heard of this term?"

"No," I had to say and gladly. "Edward Stein, our Finance professor, is new and he probably hasn't learned the Finance faculty jargon yet."

"Well," she continued, "my favorite is 'milk and slaughter.' That's the strategy for buying a company, 'milking' its assets, and then selling the leftovers."

I thought the terms were gruesome but probably accurate descriptions of what occurred in many acquisitions. Our conversation brought back the analytic structure we had just learned in Business Policy. The structure came from the Boston Consulting Group—specialists in formulating company strategy. They had developed a portfolio concept that a company could use to look at its businesses.

A four-block matrix was drawn; the left and top sides were labeled Growth and Market Share, and the blocks were labeled High and Low.

		MARKET SHARE	
		Low	High
GROWTH	Low	dog	cash cow
	High	question mark	star

A company put each of its businesses in the block corresponding to the growth potential and the amount of market share it had. Businesses that were high growth and high share were called *stars;* they were the parts of a company that should be invested in because they provide future profitability. The businesses in the high growth, low share block were *question marks;* no one knew what to do with them. *Dogs* was the term for low growth, low share businesses. They should be divested, according to the Boston Consulting Group model. And a business with a high share, low growth niche was a *cash cow*. It should be "milked" of money because it is so profitable.

There was something very unsavory to me about analyzing business in these terms. It sounded so mechanical, so detached, absolutely unfeeling; the animals were objects to use and throw away. It was discomforting enough to talk about animals that way, but we were also talking about products and people—executives, employees, and consumers—in that absolutely analytical fashion. It was heady, elegant analysis, but somehow dangerous and susceptible to abuse; we never discussed that aspect. Somehow I couldn't bring myself to comment on discussions in Business Policy when we milked cows.

When I thought about portfolio analysis and cash cows, I wondered if I was too sensitive and took things too seriously or the wrong way. I questioned myself often, but I couldn't dispel the feeling that the self-confidence I possessed when I had come into school was being eroded by the process of being there. I couldn't escape feeling as though women in the corporations we studied and women in school were not viewed as equals to men. Even with our HBS training, I knew we were not and never would be one of the good old boys who got and kept power. It was never clearer to me than on the day we had a union-management negotiation in Human Resources Management.

It was a group assignment and the section was split into teams. Kate, Danielle Murray, and Pat Worth were assigned to a team with Guillermo Davila and Paul Hedeman. They were the union team and had either to negotiate a new wage agreement or strike. The management team included Stan Hooper. Each team had time to develop a package of demands and determine its compromise position. Danielle, Kate, and Pat worked hard with their team, but they found their confidence shaken when the teams filed into the conference room, sat down, and Stan started the session with, "How nice of you boys to have brought your wives along."

Good old Stan. We could depend on him to let us know where we really stood. Danielle and Pat were steaming mad even days later, and we decided to invite our HRM professor, Roger Winchester, to our WSA lunch to talk it over. Nearly every woman in the class came to that WSA meeting, even women who had never come and didn't belong to the organization. Most of us were curious about how Roger would answer our questions.

At our lunch we didn't have much time to eat because we were so interested in the discussion. First we talked about HRM, and then more generally about HBS and what it is like to be women in large corporations. Roger confirmed our expectations.

"It's not any easier working than it is at school," he said. "A lot of people still don't accept women as decision makers; they're afraid women in executive posts will portray weakness at the top of an organization. The attitude Kate, Pat, and Danielle found in their union negotiation is more true in the outside world than not. Still, it is changing, and you'll find it easier than women even a few years before you."

We asked if he thought we had to change ourselves, make ourselves more like male executives, if we wanted to succeed in male-dominated companies. Roger said he thought not, and he certainly hoped not.

I was pleased with our exchange with Roger Winchester. It was the first time I had sat down with a group of HBS students and talked informally with a faculty member. It felt so good that I asked Danielle to arrange another WSA lunch and invited Dickson Grant, our BGIE professor, to talk with us. Dickson was an HBS graduate of 1980, and Danielle and I thought his view of corporations from a younger vantage point would complement Roger's more experienced view.

We were right because the women who came to lunch with Dickson asked him not about corporations but about relationships with men.

Sheryl Shaw spoke up first. "Dickson, you're only slightly older than we are. You've been through HBS and you worked for a consulting firm. Now you're a professor here. What do you think of women students here, and why is it so hard for us to meet and date men?"

There was so much about Dickson Grant that I loved at that moment. He was secure enough to put aside his role as a professor and just talk. So few faculty or administrators at school seemed capable of doing that.

"The choices are very tough," he said. "I dated a woman at school who graduated a year before I did. We agreed that I would travel to New York, where she worked, while I was in my second year at school. Well, I was president of the student body during my second year and I didn't get to New York very often. I lost her and I've regretted it ever since. What I'm trying to say is that you'll come out of Harvard hard-charging. You want a career, a good one, with a lot of perks and promotions. The toll is to be taken in your time, though. Good relationships take time and so do good careers. It's very hard to have both people in a relationship seeking high-paying, demanding careers. Most of the men in this school want those careers and they want women who will complement their lifestyle, not challenge it."

Irene Lenkowski spoke next. I was surprised by her presence at the meeting. Irene was the only woman student in Section D who was older than I. She was in her late thirties and had worked in sales for IBM for the previous ten years. Irene had an eighteen-month-old baby boy, John. How could she manage HBS, a baby, and a husband? She didn't attend any WSA activities and it was unusual that she had come to our lunches with Roger and now Dickson. I watched her intensely and wondered what she'd say.

"There's another side to the issue of women and careers," Irene said. "You know that at IBM I was the head of a sales and marketing department. I hired and promoted salesmen all the time. It was very hard to find women whose careers I wanted to develop, because I could count on men devoting one hundred fifty percent of their time to IBM. Women just didn't. They seemed to believe responsibilities at home are just as important. When they take time out for children, it's even more disruptive."

"What about your choice to have John?" I asked.

"I went right back to work," Irene said. "I don't think babies need motherly attention as much as everyone thinks."

"But what about those of us who want to spend some time with our children?" Sheryl asked.

"I don't think you can expect corporations to treat you the same way they treat men," Irene said.

The room was silent and the dark, paneled walls, mahogany conference table, and padded leather chairs added an almost surrealistic tone to our discussion. Dickson Grant wasn't even in the conversation now and he sat back watching us.

I didn't like the gist of Irene's point and said so. "Nothing will change for women unless we break the stereotype of what a good career requires," I said. "I believe it is just as deadly for men to be expected to put in one hundred fifty percent for the company as it is for women. Men suffer, too, from the lack of rest and full family life. They get ulcers, they get heart attacks, and they die young, leaving widows with lonely retirement years. If women do what men do, forfeiting the personal side of their lives, then where will we be?"

Our discussion led nowhere because we were struggling with issues that had no final resolution. As we got up to head back to class, Danielle announced that since it was April, our next lunch would be the last WSA meeting for the year. I knew I would miss the meetings. I needed the laughter we shared when we talked about our experiences. I needed to feel as though I wasn't the only one with a certain point of view. Each time I talked about my feelings, I was able to get the support I needed to struggle a little bit harder. Sarah Ann suggested that our last meeting be a free-for-all.

"Bring your best story for the year and we'll take a vote on which one is the most outlandish," she said.

How could we go wrong? I knew we'd have a great lunch.

The next weeks seemed to whiz by. I found I had more perspective on my surroundings, probably because I had a better idea of whether I'd be allowed to continue the program and get my degree. The immediacy of having to perform or flunk was gone. I felt a sense of liberation, as though I were now free to learn just for me. On the other hand, my more relaxed view of the HBS system allowed me to see the pressure and stress more clearly. It surfaced in bizarre ways and let me know that none of us could quite let down our defenses and be easygoing about classes or cases.

Thomas Rhinehart was a case in point. By now, most of us had a good grasp of what marketing was about. But Thomas still seemed wound up, trying to prove how much he, as a professor, was in control. One afternoon in late April we studied the K-B Mushroom case. The problem in the case was a thorny one; the domestic mushroom market was being eaten away by international competition. How could K-B, an American company, differentiate itself from all the rest when most consumers didn't notice gradations in quality between stems, buttons, and pieces of mushroom?

The class began with Thomas introducing Professor Abraham Heywood, the head of the Marketing department, with flowery praise. I found it embarrassing because I didn't care much for the Marketing department, or at least the part of it that I had experienced. That week the school newspaper had featured Professor Heywood in an article about how Marketing fit into our first-year education. He was supportive of the system, particularly the forced Low Pass and screen grading process, and he was quoted as saying that the unworkable load was a positive way to bring the best out in students. I thought his view was bunk and was skeptical of the praise he was getting from Thomas. Professor Heywood was apparently in class to observe Thomas's teaching methods and he was busy writing notes as soon as class began.

It turned out to be a banner day for observing Thomas Rhinehart. Halfway into class, Richard Travis raised his hand and offered his analysis on the future of the domestic mushroom market. After he stopped talking, Thomas spun around and said, "And where do you get support for that position, Richard?"

"From the ten percent market share growth I saw in the case," Richard said.

Thomas moved fast. He flew up to where Richard sat on the skydeck and stood in front of his desk.

"That number is wrong," Thomas said. "If you look at page three, paragraph two, the last line, you will see that market share growth is two, not ten, percent. Your position can't be supported with case facts."

Rich's face flushed red, his body slumped in his seat. The rest of us twitched uneasily. I seethed as I watched Thomas pick on Rich, and seethed too at Abraham Heywood for being the kind of department head who probably relished behavior of this sort by members of the faculty. The class ended in an atmosphere of apprehension; Thomas had lost a lot of support from students because of his behavior.

Last fall I might have visited Thomas in his office and

talked over the incident, trying to find out why class was so tense and why he was so brutal. Now I didn't care enough to do anything; the system drained away whatever concern I might have had for him. What I felt instead was frustration at how little anyone seemed to care about the students.

In Production and Operations Management, for example, I took a morning off from class the day after I opened the New Balance case. I took it off because I was getting a cold and knew the night before that if I went to bed early and slept late I wouldn't get sick. If I didn't take it easy I'd probably get the cold and feel badly for a week. It was the only morning I had taken off since the day I studied for Control before Thanksgiving vacation.

The next morning I had another POM class, and as I headed out my door, Sarah Ann called to ask if I would tell Duke Moore before class that she wouldn't be in. She was exhausted and felt some kind of bug had gotten hold of her, too.

I did tell Duke when I got to class and took the opportunity to apologize for skipping class the day before.

"Sure, I understand," he said. "I know it's the tradition to take it easy after you've been called on. And as for Sarah Ann, I'm sure she's busy with her wedding plans."

"No, that's not it," I said. "We've been sick."

He smiled and turned to answer another student's question. I went to my seat and ached. What a drag to have my professor, whose opinion I care about, think he knows me so well that he doesn't really hear what I say.

Expectations by professors played such a large role in our behavior even now, when a lot of the intense pressure was gone. It made us perform even if we didn't feel like it, even if we didn't know what we were talking about. I found myself dreaming about classes often; I was almost always saying the wrong thing or saying nothing at all. I had dreamed just the other night about Dickson Grant and my BGIE class. In the dream, I hadn't talked for days and Dickson walked up to me and said, loud enough for everyone to hear, that he was really disappointed in me. He expected more—would I talk more?

I could see the pressure on Kate and Sarah Ann and other students too. I had been dumbstruck by Kate in a Business Policy class a short time ago. The case was the chain saw industry, and we were studying the effects of skyrocketing sales of chain saws in the mid- and late-1970s. We were asked to look at the position of competitors: McCulloch, Homelite, Beard-Poulin, and Stihl and predict their responses to the slump in sales that has occurred in subsequent years.

Kate was called on to open the case and she gave what I thought was a thorough opening statement. It wasn't quite what our professor, Hugh Ostrander, had in mind, however. He wanted Kate to pin down her assumptions about market share growth for each of the competitors. When Hugh looked at Kate and asked her if she had any more numbers, she said no and then, to my wide-eyed amazement, she put both her hands together in a praying gesture and said, "Forgive."

She looked like the image of a nun in a convent, confessing to sins that didn't seem bad to me. Her gesture disturbed me, and later, when I told her that she was expecting far too much out of herself, she laughed and said she didn't remember doing it at all.

"It must have been a throwback to my old Catholic school girl days in junior high," she said. "Now, there the pressure to be good was really tough to handle. I prayed all the time back then."

By now we were taking our familiar walk across the Charles River and were heading into Harvard Square. Our conversation turned to Finance, the class both of us were struggling very hard to understand. As with our other courses, Finance required that we deal with a new concept in every class for the first half of the semester. The midterm had been hard; we were expected to do a discounted cash flow analysis, a DCF, a technique which we had had only two days of cases to learn. We had gotten Sats on the midterm, but it wasn't because we were on top of the material. We had shared my Control tutor, Reva Cromwell, and she had helped us structure our approach to the exam just enough to get us through.

"Hey, Kate," I said. "We've got to buckle down and learn DCF by the final. How are we going to do it?"

"I know it's important," Kate said. "Maybe we could have a session together with Reva and talk through once again what we don't understand."

Discounted cash flow was important. It seemed to crop up everywhere. In ME we had had to do a DCF on the midterm, but I didn't have a clue about how to use my calculator well enough to do it back then. According to our Finance professor, if we wanted to do a proper financial analysis of an investment decision, DCF was vital to the process.

The overall concept is not too tricky. It is based on the fact that one dollar in my hand today is not worth the same as one dollar at any other point in time. Inflation and the interest that I could earn on the dollar are the two major determinants of what the dollar will be worth tomorrow or ten years from now. To make a choice between two investment decisions—say, building a company from scratch, or buying one outright—requires applying this concept.

If I take these two choices, building and buying, and project all the earnings, real cash earnings, I will have a certain dollar amount at the end of each year. But I can't just add up the earnings and say that is how much I'll make, because the value of the money each year, due to interest earnings and inflation, will be different. I can discount the earnings to the present, however, and get the money's present value. Then I can compare the two decisions in like currency: today's dollars.

The tricky part of this analysis for Kate and me was in the technique of getting the cash flows right and in picking the discount rate. We had to take into account the company's cost of borrowed money, depreciation, tax factors, and inflation, and it easily became a murky process to wade through.

DCF was important to us for another reason. We had just made a big decision when we signed up for second-year courses. We both wanted to understand finance more than any other subject—and we had chosen as many courses related to it as we could fit into our schedule. We both signed up for Investment Management, rumored to be one of the hardest courses in the second-year curriculum; Analysis of Corporate Financial Reports; Capital Markets; and Corporate Financial Management. We knew we'd be in hot water for the whole year if we didn't get DCF.

Yet on some level, perhaps one deep in our unconscious, we resisted the rationality and the power of the things we were learning. As much as we wanted to understand finance, there was a pull toward the humanist, the intuitive, side, which had little to do with cash flows or discount rates. This was the side that erupted in laughter when we missed yet another key case point or when we refused to make decisions "on the numbers alone."

For me, this side got some play at our WSA lunches for it was there that I could let down and just be me. Our last lunch was scheduled for May 7, and as I sat down in the formality of the school's private dining room, I wondered what our best stories of the year would be. Here were the six women I'd gotten to know best in Section D: Sheryl Shaw, Kate, Sarah Ann, Danielle, Devaki, and Susan Mantero. Sarah Ann reminded us that at our last lunch we had said we'd bring favorite stories from the year. She started the meeting off with hers.

"Mine is from two days ago in Finance class," she said, and as she continued I could see Kate's cheeks get bright red. "I can't resist retelling it, because it says so much about where Kate's priorities are—and they aren't always rooted in DCF!"

"Edward Stein was trying to get us to understand the pressure that interest-rate fluctuations put on business. Do you remember? He was trying to get us to focus on the early nineteen seventies. Very few of us know anything about interest rates in the early seventies—after all, even Edward Stein was in high school in nineteen seventy. He finally asked a specific question, rare for him. 'What was the most important event in the spring of 1970—come on class,' is what he said. And, Kate, your answer was out of this world."

"Kent State," Kate said.

We all laughed with her, remembering that was just the way she had said it in class. Edward Stein had laughed too, and then he had told us, no, the recession of 1970 was what he had had in mind.

Kate spoke up. "Yes, that story shows where my sense of reality is. And now I'll tell you my favorite—it's about a second-year student I met when I was using the Office for Career Development. Her name is Becky Mintz; you may have seen her around campus and you couldn't miss her. In April she was nine months pregnant!

"She managed to get pregnant on schedule last summer so that she could try and give birth during spring break, and do you know—she did it. She had a baby girl the second week in April. But that's not my story.

"In March, she and I happened to be on a plane together; she'd gotten on at a stopover. Both of us had been interviewing, and even though we sat two seats apart, we couldn't help but share our experiences. Hers were far more outrageous than mine.

"Becky had just interviewed for the second time with her first-choice company and she had to meet the senior vice-president for something or other. After hello, he soon got around to her very pregnant state. He asked her what her plans were after she gave birth and she replied that she planned to take the summer off after graduation and start work in September, as was typical of most students.

"He finally spelled out what was on his mind. He asked her point-blank, 'Don't you think mothers should be home with their children?' Becky replied that she thought it was great if parents could be home with their children and that was exactly the reason why her husband would quit his job and stay home with their baby!

"Well, our section of the plane roared. There were men sitting all around us, and we didn't realize how many of them had been listening. When she got up to leave, a number of them said good luck."

Kate looked so pleased with her tale because it was a ray of hope for those of us who wanted to see some changes in the traditional way of doing things.

My story was next; unfortunately, it wasn't as hopeful as Kate's, but it was on a familiar subject—guests in class. Once or twice a week, we had guest speakers in our classes who were either individuals in the case that day or who spoke to the class from an informed perspective. While I found that on the whole professors were never sexist in their comments in class, this was not true for guests, and women were often the subject of their warmup jokes. Definitely my unfavorite example of this was from last fall, when we had a guest in a Control class, a principal in an investment banking house in Boston. He was reviewing the importance of annual reports to research analysts in investment houses. He commented on the McCormick Company, which sells spices but now has diversified into other fields.

I asked if anyone around me remembered this particular speaker. Most did, and I continued by quoting what I could from my memory.

"Remember, he picked up the annual report for McCormick, which was on the desk—he sniffed it. He said it smelled like some spice, he didn't know which, maybe cinnamon or ginger. He said McCormick had started to scent its reports a few years ago. When they did, it started a big rush among research analysts. They were all calling up Frederick's of Hollywood, hoping that McCormick had started a trend and they could be the first to get a good sniff of Frederick's annual report."

"Oh groan," Sarah Ann said. "I do remember that but I'd blocked it completely. It made me feel awful, like sitting in class with everyone laughing at you."

We didn't laugh; we just breathed deeply and wondered why women were called girls when it was actually the men around us who wouldn't grow up.

Susan Mantero offered the last story. Again I was surprised by her comments, as I had been at our very first lunch. She didn't have a story as much as a criticism.

She said, "I just got a copy of the Section D picture book. The skydeck people have been working on it for the past month, getting photographs of Section D and putting together captions."

Susan turned and looked at Danielle.

"Danielle," she said, "I know you put a lot of work in it. You're really one of the boys up there on the skydeck. It seems like the skydeck was trying to get back at the section somehow and that book is very insulting to women. The picture of Sheryl Shaw propositioning two professors was a cheap shot and I didn't like it. In fact, I wish I'd never seen it."

I had seen the book and had to agree with Susan.

As we got up from our last lunch together, we acknowledged how very hard it was to be our old selves in the HBS environment and said we wished we didn't feel the pressure the way we did. It sometimes brought out the worst in us, hardly fitting for the country's best school of management.

It was the end of May now, and the last week of classes and exams were upon us. We began, one by one, to say goodbye to professors. There was a tradition for it. If we liked the professor, we wrote a poem or song and clapped as class ended. We did this for each one except Margaret Price. Some sections bought gifts for professors, but we weren't so demonstrative. Duke Moore was the class favorite: we gave him a big bouquet of tiger lilies.

When we said goodbye to Thomas Rhinehart, it felt painful. Instead of ending the class early, he talked nervously about classroom strategy from the professor's point of view. Finally he started to leave and we sang a song for him. Instead of walking out as the applause started, the way the other professors had, he stood there and took it in, nervous as ever—which confused us. Were we supposed to keep on until he finally got the hint and left or stop in case he wanted to talk? It was an appropriately awkward ending for Marketing with Thomas Rhinehart.

The farewell to Margaret Price could have been voted my most unpleasant experience of the year. Margaret couldn't come to the last class because of an illness in her family. This was a very rare event—professors always came to class. She did, however, send a videotape to say goodbye. When Rick Cabot turned the lights down and Margaret came on the screen, some of the men started booing and laughing. Then they crumpled up paper and threw it at her image. She deserved more respect, and I left the room.

The exam schedule was posted, and as before, we had exams the day after school ended. I was nervous, but not in a panicked way. Now I wanted a chance to show myself how much I had learned.

Our Marketing final was first and it made me as mad as the midterm. First, I was mad because of the product. The midterm had been about an industrial product that I didn't understand; the final was a consumer good—silverware. We were asked to work up a marketing strategy for selling flatware to the "prebridal" group. The case had been written in 1957 and was so limited in its view of young married people that I found it impossible to relate to. When I got out of the exam, I was even madder to discover that the critical calculation in the case was a breakeven analysis that was done perfectly and printed in our *Note on Breakeven Analysis,* a reference pamphlet given to us in the first week of school. Some students had just copied the example from the *Note* into their exam books. There was nothing dishonorable about it; the fault was in the Marketing department.

In Business Policy a similar thing occurred. Our exam was on Prelude, a company that harvested and sold lobsters. We were asked to comment and design a strategy for them. It turned out that an analysis of where Prelude had gone wrong was in Michael Porter's *Competitive Strategy,* the hottest selling book on campus. Porter was a professor who taught in second year and many students had bought and read his book in anticipation of his class next year.

In contrast, my favorite exam was BGIE; we were given Ronald Reagan's State of the Union address and asked to analyze it from an economic perspective. Was it economically and politically feasible to do what he said he would do? I enjoyed the exam and as a result did what I thought was a good job. I knew, too, that I couldn't have commented on Reagan's policies from an economic perspective before HBS, and it was a good feeling to see some value in my training.

Finance was the last and it was a killer. Kate, Sarah Ann, Joyce, and I went to lunch at Ferdinand's afterward. We needed a glass of wine and a million slices of chocolate cheesecake. We weren't sure what was going on and we were tremendously keyed up.

Our emotion stemmed from the exam and from the experience of the whole year. We had sat in the Finance final, our last test in an unbelievable string of obstacles, confronted with a case miles away from what we had studied during the semester. It was part of the professor's strategy to give a very hard exam, one that would stretch us, so the bell curve of our grades would be broadened. That made it easy to distinguish Low Passes from Sats and Sats from E's. It might have been easy for them, but it was destructive to us because we hovered too near the screen already and one flunked Finance exam might push us right over the edge.

We settled down to toast the school year—it was over! Then who should walk into Ferdinand's but Edward Stein and the whole first-year Finance faculty. We stared him down until he averted his eyes and put his arms over his head to protect himself. They were laughing all through lunch; we were sure we'd flunked Finance. But after a while we laughed and relaxed too; we were so relieved that our first year was over!

Two weeks later I was back in Washington, D.C.—free of cases for the summer and full of plans for our business. It was almost a shock to get my white envelope from Harvard with my first-year grades. There they were in the familiar computer typeface. I wasn't scared, as I had been in March. Now I just felt simple relief and a little pride:

Control	S
Managerial Economics	LP
Organizational Behavior	E
Management Communications	E
Human Relations Management	S
Production and Operations Management	S
Business, Government, and the International Economy	E
Finance	S
Business Policy	S
Marketing	S

My pride was mixed with bitterness as I thought of those of my colleagues who had been sweating out their grades until June 15 and would now find out they couldn't go back to school. I was okay, but it wasn't quite enough—what about the others? The angry feelings I had about school, the intimidation—it all seemed worth it because I had gotten through. I knew it must be hell for them.

I put my grades away and headed into summer. Next September was eons away and I hoped to relish every moment until then.

7

COASTING AND CRASHING

Last year on the first day of school I wore a new skirt and a blue oxford shirt to class; today I have on jeans, a T-shirt, and my purple backpack. My joy is unbounded. I'm no longer a first-year student. The only reason I am sure is because everywhere there are strangers on campus and they look nervous and very well dressed. I certainly don't envy them, and my strongest emotion is relief.

The same feeling comes back day after day as I begin my new courses. I can't quite believe it—I'm not a first-year student anymore. It takes class after class to sink in. The terrible pressure of the screen or of just doing poorly, embarrassment at not knowing what to say in class, the dead weight of not understanding everything, the insecurity that comes with not feeling good about yourself—all of it is gone.

Second year is like first year in that we still do cases every night and many professors cold-call students. Everything else has changed. There is only one required course, Business

Policy II, and in that course we don't sit with our old section mates. Harvard did that until just a few years ago but the students, full of self-confidence and bold when sitting with their old section mates, apparently tore apart the BP professors. Now BP II class, like my five other classes, is filled with strangers, with only a small sprinkling of Section D's familiar faces. Sarah Ann's is one such face.

On the first day we sat next to each other, in the second row. This class was smaller than a typical one from last year and no one sat in the first row, so we were in plain view of the professor. I shocked myself and Sarah Ann, too, when I slipped her a note. In all of first year I'd passed notes only once or twice. Back then I was too absorbed in everything else that was going on.

I asked her to meet me for lunch if she could. She wrote back making a date for later in the week. I wanted to see her soon, but I was pleased for the delay because I had to think about what to say.

During the summer Sarah Ann's mother had died very unexpectedly, a few days before Sarah Ann's June wedding. When I had first heard about it I was in shock, and on the few occasions I had talked with her in July and August I couldn't manage to say what I wanted. There was something about Sarah Ann's mother dying that changed me. It made me think about the few times in the last year when reality had intruded on my one-dimensional life.

There was election night, when Ronald Reagan won the presidency and I cried with my Washington, D.C., friends over all that would follow during his administration. We saw budget cuts for our important programs and rough times ahead for the Equal Rights Amendment. And in early December John Lennon was killed; I cried then, too, for this sensitive man who symbolized a lot when I was growing up and who left behind a grieving family. Then, in May, the

Pope was shot and it seemed crazy I was living in a world unable to handle even its spiritual leaders.

But the death of Sarah Ann's mother awakened me to something closer to home. It made me think of being thirty-three and of my priorities. I vowed to myself, once again, that however hard Harvard tried to be the number one priority in my life, it would not happen. Resisting the pressure took more guts than I realized. Last year there had been the temptation to do more work when I needed instead to relax and play, listen to music, or talk to friends. The lack of confidence that each of us felt going through the program hounded us into doing more, and it became a psychological struggle to carve out space and time for the other-than-Harvard parts of us. When I sat in BP II class and thought about Sarah Ann, I wanted to tell her these things and I knew I would later in the week. In the meantime, we wrote notes back and forth for most of our three BP classes.

Business Policy II, like my other courses, had the promise of being an exciting learning experience. BP II took off from BP I, which was aimed at teaching us how to identify corporate strategy. BP II's goal was to teach us how to put strategy into action. On the one hand, that meant dealing with the buzz words I disliked so—*cash cow, dog,* and *milk and slaughter.* On the other hand, I could see in the schedule that two weeks were dedicated to discussions of ethical issues in corporate strategy. I was curious to discover how these issues would be handled, and I thought, How quaint; two weeks out of two years.

True, we had had a case on ethics in BP I. The case was the Reserve Mining Company of Minnesota and we had discussed the pros and cons of dumping taconite tailings into the bay that fed Duluth's water supply. And in Production and Operations Management and Marketing we had once discussed ethical issues in a roundabout yes-let's-get-this-discussion-over-with way.

The Management Communications faculty felt it necessary to discuss ethics in nearly every case, but the effect of it was meaningless, since we weren't expected to take MC seriously. The class discussions tended to get off the track of teaching us good writing and speaking skills and made many students angry at MC. In summary, our first-year ethics discussions left a lot to be desired.

Before I came to the school, I was intrigued by how ethics would be treated at Harvard and I was curious about the points of view of my colleagues, the future business leaders of the world. Holly Winthrop told me not to expect much. One of her professors, in introducing the "ethics segment" in class, had said that he thought it was a waste to devote a lot of time to the subject. "If the students don't have ethical points of view before they get to school," he had said, "they won't develop them in this class." And ethical behavior was expected out of Harvard's students a priori.

With reasoning like that, I wondered why we were taught anything at school; after all, I hadn't known discounted cash flow or how to segment a market before coming to school, either. Nevertheless, we'd finally discuss ethical issues in BP II and I looked forward to it.

I was full of excitement for my other courses too. There was so much I still didn't understand from first year. I hadn't yet put together all of the concepts I had learned—like what it meant to squeeze gross margin in order to give retailers a better cut and what that implied for profits. And I was far from understanding what people meant when they said that short-term interest rates should be less than long-term ones and that the economy suffered now from an inverted yield curve.

It was rumored among many second-year students that this year would be a complete bore—the only things that kept them in classes were the requirement that we get a certain number of Sats and the promise of getting a job in the spring. It wouldn't be that way for me, I knew. I wanted time in classes and time to do cases, without the pressure of the screen—more time to simply learn.

Yet one week into the year I was unnerved by my decision last spring to tackle hard courses because so much of what I had to learn in second year seemed over my head. Investment Management was the hardest course. On the first day, our professor, Gabriel Doucette, announced that the course was not for people who were interested in personal investments. Investment Management was designed for students who wanted to work in finance, managing large portfolios of money. The course curriculum, predictably, covered three areas—bonds, stocks, and options. We were to learn about bond prices, especially the current violent and untraditional behavior of bond prices, and how to judge risk among different bond sellers. We would tackle the art of valuing stock—how we could tell whether a stock was a good or poor buy. Options were also on the schedule. People who bought and sold in the options market tried to predict short-term price swings in stocks. It sounded scary as hell to me.

While on the first day of Investment Management class there were people sitting in the aisles, by the next class our ranks had thinned to fifty people or so. I shouldn't be here, I thought. I don't know what he's talking about, ever. But I stuck with it—every day being as hard as the last. Each night I struggled with Investment Management—maybe, if I just concentrated hard enough, I'd get it.

I was nervous about the course mainly because I hadn't been given my choice in getting the second-year finance background course, Corporate Financial Management. In order to get into courses, each student had to give a list of priorities to the registrar. CFM was my second priority, and because so many other students had made it their first priority, I didn't get in. As a result I was taking Investment Management and Capital Markets without the security of what I perceived to be a more fundamental course.

Capital Markets turned out to be great. It was taught by Stephen Smith, a delightfully humorous man who announced on the first day of classes that he wouldn't call on people to open. What a blessing. That, coupled with the subject matter, allowed me to enjoy going to class. In Capital Markets we would learn how to understand the current situation of banks and how the savings and loans institutions were being squeezed by high interest rates. We would also study how interest rates were structured and theories about what caused high or low rates. We dabbled in understanding commodities trading and Federal Reserve policies, among other things.

I also signed up for Retailing, Management of Operations, and the Management of Small Business. I was lucky to get Retailing. It was taught by an outstanding professor, Kami Ito, and I knew I'd love the course from the first day because Kami's first gesture was to crack some funny jokes and make us all feel at home in his class. There would be pressure to talk and he would cold-call us, he announced, but I could tell he had none of the sadism in his manner that had been typical in my dealings with the Marketing department.

Second-year professors were under pressure in a way that first year ones were not. After a course was over, each student rated his or her professor on a five-point scale for ten or so criteria. The results were tabulated and published in computer printouts for the following year's second-year students to use in selecting their professors. Harvard took the student rankings seriously, and tenure decisions were made partly on this basis.

Students used the rankings to zero in on the best professors, assuming that since marketing, finance, and operations were related, a lot of the courses would be similar. Because of this combination of factors, the second-year faculty tended to be more renowned in their fields, have more in-class experience, and be more interested in students' evaluations of their teaching skills.

Two of the most popular courses on campus were Management of Small Business and Real Estate. Hundreds more signed up for these courses than could get in. It surprised the administration that this was so, but they didn't hire any more professors to fill the gap, leaving many disgruntled students. This was the case for Kate, who planned to work in real estate development and who hadn't gotten in even though she had given the real estate course her number one priority.

We met outside Aldrich to talk about how we were doing. One week into our schedule and already tired, we found it hard to be mellow, as we had hoped we would be in second year.

"I don't know what the problem is," Kate said. "I came to school with this course in mind. It makes me so mad that I can't use what I've learned in my summer job."

"I know what you mean; I didn't get into CFM and it scares me to death to be in two other finance courses without it," I said.

We both were taking Investment Management but were in different sections. In fact, we had no classes together, so we'd have to arrange our meeting times or we wouldn't see each other all semester. Just as we started discussing Gabriel Doucette and Investment Management, we were interrupted by Richard Travis and Michael Mitchell. We hadn't seen either of them since last spring.

"Hey, what happened to Rudolf Ziegler?" Rich said, talking to Kate. "He was in your study group, wasn't he? I looked at our second-year mail boxes, but didn't see his name or Tony Giambelli's either. Did they decide to take a year off?"

Kate looked at me with a look I'd learned to translate—Rich Travis, you're a jerk, she was thinking.

"I guess so," she said. "Rudolf got a job in London and didn't want to continue the program this year. I don't know what happened to Tony."

We all knew what had happened to Tony, and to Rudolf Ziegler and Ron Watts too. They had hit the screen. Rudolf and Tony had been asked to take some extra courses and come back another time. Ron had been asked to leave outright.

Kate and I left the campus tired of the whole process and sick at heart thinking of the gleam in Rich Travis's eye when he asked if "Rudolf took the year off." Rich Travis was a nice guy last year, what the hell happened to him?

We talked about Rudolf and Ron for a while. We knew them pretty well; they had sat right in front of us, and Rudolf had been in Kate's study group. They had worked very hard; it seemed so unfair. The problem was that they hadn't talked. It wasn't that they had given up, as the faculty would have us believe. But even though we felt badly about their fate, if it hadn't been them, who would it have been? The whole crummy system stank.

"Kate, I feel like a coward. I can't change the system—I just feel incredible relief that I'm not a first-year student anymore."

"Don't worry, the school wants you to feel that way. By the time we're alumnae we'll have rationalized it all away," Kate said.

Then she burst out laughing. It was a joke, we knew,

because it wouldn't be true for us. We'd never gloss over how we felt last year.

"Hey, we're not the only ones who feel some pain left from last year," Kate said. "Did you see the *Harbus News* today?"

I hadn't, and she pulled out her copy. I read Danielle Murray's letter to the editor about last spring's Marketing final. I thought it superb:

Hesper Silver

> To the editors:
>
> I tried running four miles a day. I tried drinking four times a day. I tried waiting four months. But I'm still angry. I still need to tell the Marketing Department where they can stick and keep their ludicrous final. The Hesper Silver Company.
>
> For those unfamiliar with the Hesper Silver Company, here are a couple of pearls from this 1957 case about selling silverware to women—a case that reflects values most women at Harvard struggle to transcend.
>
> a. "Concentrate on the young prebridal group, the girl who is still dreaming, planning, hoping . . ."
>
> b. "Let the contemporary housewife feel comfortable when her table is set with sterling, a sign of her success as a modern wife, woman, and hostess."
>
> Obviously the Marketing Department didn't consider how women in 1981 might feel taking this exam. No doubt we were to ignore our convictions and silly emotions, and act like real business-

> men. They justified this ancient piece saying, "It is truly a classic case, and has played a critical role as the opening or closing of first-year Marketing." Wrong. It isn't critical. It isn't even a learning experience. And it hurts.
>
> Actually, the case itself was no more irritating than waiting for one of two bathroom stalls during the same damn exam, while staring at no less than six urinals. But some things have changed. The urinals were removed over the summer and I applaud the enlightened behavior of the Maintenance Department. Let's let them choose the Marketing final this year.
>
> Danielle Murray

"It's going to be a trying year, from our woman's point of view," Kate said. "Look at this letter, it says it all. The frustration of feeling like you don't fit in. The anger that comes from not being listened to. This year we don't have our Section D WSA group—we'll have to make up our own."

"Definitely," I said. "Hey, that reminds me, did you know that Susan Mantero got married over the summer and is spending this year in Chicago? Her husband applied here but didn't get in. She's decided to wait another year for him to try again and then she'll get her degree. Can you imagine a man doing that for a woman? I hope such a man exists; I just haven't met any."

"Neither have any of the women here," Kate said. "You know Dorothy Henderson, the president of the Student Association? In Retailing class she announced that she and a friend had T-shirts for sale to the women on campus. The shirts say 'Love Me Till Graduation.' They are in recognition that school is so hard, and finding men who take us seriously is impossible. Dorothy and her friend knew there would be a market for the T-shirts, and I think they were right."

What conflicts I felt at Harvard in the fall of 1981. Looking at the school from the outside, even I would be impressed. The president of the Student Association was a woman, the editor and the publisher of the school newspaper were both women, the president of the Venture Capital Club and the Political Forum Club were women. Women were also presidents of the Marketing, Energy Resources Management, Computer Industry and Technology, and the Engineering and Technology Management Clubs. Women were also active in regional and ethnic clubs, and of course women were heads of the Women's Student Association and the HBS Partner's Club.

But life on a personal plane was not as impressive, and I knew it would take as much courage to get through this year as it had the last. First, there was our assignment in Small Business class. We had a case book entitled "Who Are the Entrepreneurs?" The article was written in 1974 by a former HBS professor and I didn't expect quite the jolt I got when I read it.

The answer to the question posed in the title "Who Are the Entrepreneurs?" was a chapter's worth of how "he sees himself ready" and "how many distractions or obligations he sees holding him back." One such obligation is the

> typical male life cycle development in the United States between 25 and 40. A man gets married, buys a house, and starts to raise a family. He may immediately incur a sizable mortgage and real estate taxes. With children he acquires the cost burdens for their future education. In addition, he assumes responsibility for his family in the event of his death or disability. . . . Other commitments

> created by marriage and families may do as much to restrict the freedom and flexibility of would-be entrepreneurs as do financial obligations. Few women marry with the intention of becoming nurses and housecleaners for absentee husbands. Moreover, personal relationships among people require time . . .

The description went on for pages; it was rooted in the past and had little relevance to the world I lived in. Where were the women entrepreneurs and where were the women who worked and shared family responsibilities? Where were the men who wanted a family life and a new business? Where were the business people for whom family life is not a burden but rather a joy—in fact possibly more important than getting to the top. The common assumption made by this professor was that people could not devote quality time to a family and start a business too. How deadly, I thought, and how unfair to exact such a commitment from an entrepreneur. Perhaps the book wouldn't have bothered me if the professor hadn't left Harvard the year before and started a venture capital company. Now he was in the position of making decisions on who gets money and I disliked his criteria immensely.

I weathered Small Business class the day after reading that case mainly because I spoke to our professor and he acknowledged the archaic opinions in our book and asked students when he started class if they would give him names of women entrepreneurs about whom the department could write cases. Out of the thirty or so cases we would read in the course only one was about a woman.

Soon after this Small Business class, I had Retailing, in which we discussed the in-store merchandising strategy of Nieman Marcus. We had a guest, a former HBSer who was head of the department that handled merchandising for the Dallas headquarters store. She brought one of her special assistants with her, a man who looked five years her senior. The class discussed the Nieman Marcus case for sixty minutes; then our professor asked our guest to come to the front of the room and comment on the discussion. She wouldn't come to the front of the room. She said she preferred talking from her skydeck seat.

I didn't blame her; I remembered how unnerving it had been to stand in front of the class for my MC speech. The class thought she should have shown how tough she was by doing it when she didn't want to, but I didn't see why she had to prove herself to us or to anyone. And, she gave a good talk from her seat.

When it came time for her colleague to speak, the class told him to come down. He refused; students booed and hissed. The student sitting next to me said, "Prove you're a man," under his breath. He still refused to come down in front of us; he had no wish to embarrass his boss.

But I thought—damn, this is too much. If the situation were reversed and the woman came down in front of the class when her male boss wouldn't, she'd be denounced as an aggressive bitch. But he's a coward because he didn't show her up.

Ah gee, the semester would be a long one, after all.

By November I was deep into my course work. The outside world was blocked out again, only rattled temporarily by Anwar Sadat's assassination. It was strange that nothing short of tragedy could get me to focus on events outside of school. My resolve to pay attention to other-than-Harvard was eroded as I grappled with Investment Management and Capital Markets.

Because I knew I'd never go through a degree program

again, I wanted to get everything out of school that I could. And the more I read the *Wall Street Journal* and the articles we were assigned on the Federal Reserve, the more I understood interest rates and the economy. It was a very heady feeling, although it wasn't knowledge I cared to impress anyone with. It was purely for my own satisfaction—finally I understood how things worked.

I began to piece things together that I hadn't been able to connect before. Like buying stock. Before Harvard I didn't pay any attention to my finances; my money sat in a bank, in a five percent savings account. But shortly before school I decided to put money in a money market fund, one that bought only government securities. It was paying fourteen percent interest at the time and the fund had check-writing privileges. At the same time I decided to buy some stock, just to see what would happen to it. On a tip from a friend in D.C., I bought some shares in a company whose stock, it was rumored, would shortly split. This meant that the stock price had gotten too high and the company would give each shareholder two or more shares for each share owned. Great, I thought; I bought.

Not long into Finance class last year, however, I had heard Edward Stein say that stock splits are meaningless. They don't change the value of your stock. I hoped he was wrong and looked up stock splits in my *Corporate Finance* book. It looked like he was right. The graph on stock splits showed that the only time a stock increases in value on a split is just before it splits, not after, because some people buy the stock (like me, I thought), causing a run-up in price which dissipates as soon as the stock splits. The underlying value of the stock hasn't changed, so the stock won't be worth any more. That means I may have bought at a high price, I thought. But I hoped not, because after all I had a tip from a friend whose opinion I trusted.

By the fall of 1981 I had owned the shares for eighteen months and had learned a lot more about stocks, all of which was bad for my meager little purchase. The most important thing I learned was that people like me, individuals with limited knowledge of Wall Street, could not expect to make a killing in the stock market. We can't expect to increase our investment more than the stock market as a whole increases. There were too many smart people out there analyzing what was going on—and I wasn't one of them. It was the old efficient markets hypothesis.

Another thing I learned was: buy stocks for a long-term investment. I learned this lesson very well because I needed to sell my stock to pay spring tuition. When I sold it, the stock market was in a slump; I lost one quarter of the value of my purchase when I sold it. Not bad for an HBSer trying to understand finance!

I was learning some other things too. By November I had some time to reflect more on the educational process at Harvard. Since so much of our case discussion now was not nitty-gritty detail work but strategy, we had time in class and out of it to be more philosophical.

During this time I read an article for my Management of Operations course entitled "Managing Our Way To Economic Decline," by two Harvard professors, Robert Hayes and William Abernathy. The article was causing a great stir on campus, a stir I was only partly aware of, since it was upsetting the faculty and I had no time to follow what was going on with them. To me the article made good common sense. Abernathy and Hayes contended that American businesses pay too much attention to making money in the short term, by squeezing profit from old production processes. They don't invest money in new plants, equipment, and methods. In the long term, managers are worse off because they have outdated production processes but don't care because bonuses are based on short-term, not long-term, financial results.

For Abernathy and Hayes, the problem is good old-fashioned discounted cash flow, the tool we used in Finance, because DCF makes it deceptively easy to decide on the numbers. They also criticized the financial ratio return on investment because it doesn't reflect value in long-term business goals.

Well, if Abernathy and Hayes were right, then a lot of what we learned at school was irrelevant and would have to be changed. First, there was Managerial Economics, which taught us that numbers are the only things that matter in business decisions. Then there was Control, in which we learned how to set up profit centers and measure performance on a short-term, return-on-investment basis. Finally, there was the whole case system. How could we learn to see problems in a long-range perspective when we dealt with eight hundred problems for three hours each? The case method encouraged short-range thinking because it set us up to analyze and solve a problem without having to account for the impact of our decisions.

Looking at my education in this light, it was no surprise to see United States industries like the automotive industry suffering with long-term quality control problems. Top executives didn't value quality because they weren't measured on it, and they didn't care enough to see that the work force was evaluated on it. Managers of companies cared much more about how many cars they could make than about the quality of those cars because the more cars they could make, the more their bonuses would be.

Woven into this problem was the often heard rationale that managers of American businesses rely on short-term financial yardsticks because Wall Street demands it. Our sophisticated stock market makes investment analysts seek the most money for their clients—the people or institutions who own the corporations. And the public, it is said, doesn't care about long-term goals or gains. It cares about how much its stock will increase in value this year.

I had a hard time figuring out which was the chicken and which was the egg. Did Harvard Business School, with its emphasis on eight hundred cases and short-term solutions, cause an overreliance on short-term objectives in the biggest U.S. companies and Wall Street investment houses? Or was it that this was the way business was structured and thus Harvard, being closely tied to business, followed suit? I didn't know the answer—but I did know that the case method had been taught at Harvard for more than fifty years and that surveys showed nineteen percent of the top three managers in the largest Fortune 500 companies had been educated at Harvard Business School. It made me suspicious of the business school as a culprit.

Maybe because of my background in social science, I was preoccupied with these things for a long time. In the meanwhile, school was moving right along. Before I knew it first-semester courses were drawing to a close and exams were upon us. There were no midterms in second year, only finals, which were half our grade; talking in class made up the other half. Some courses also required papers and presentations.

Sarah Ann, Kate, Danielle, and I got together every few weeks. We had hardly any courses together—Sarah Ann was concentrating in computers and Danielle avoided Marketing altogether. Each time we four sat down to talk, we expressed our relief that we were second-year students and we were almost out. Then we'd get down to business and tell stories about classes and courses. By now school was less demanding, and we talked about other things in our lives too.

By the time exams were upon us in mid-December, we were getting tired of working every night. We skipped a few nights' cases and shopped for the holidays or ate dinner together. One night we planned to go to Simmons College and listen to a lecture by a woman who was a partner in TA Associates, a Boston venture capital company. The speaker was a graduate of Simmons College Graduate School of Management and she was speaking on how she made partner at TA Associates in just a few years.

On the night we were to go, Sarah Ann and Kate had conflicts, so I headed off to Simmons College alone. It was a strange feeling because it was the first time I'm embarrassed to admit, that I had gone to downtown Boston on a school night since coming to school. I was very curious about Simmons College. The school had an intensive one-year MBA program which trained women for middle and upper management slots. It was a long time since I'd been in a predominantly female classroom and I wondered how it would feel.

It didn't take long to figure out; it was wonderful. The women who greeted me at the door were gracious and welcoming; for some reason they knew I was from HBS, and they asked a lot of typical questions. But when we settled down and started to listen to Jacqueline Morby, I realized what I didn't have at Harvard. This woman, probably in her early forties, had graduated from Simmons only a few years ago and had returned to school because her children were grown and she wanted a career. She was successful by anyone's standards and had the grace and command that I'd come to expect from executives.

But she wasn't trained at Harvard, and lucky for her. She had no bravado to defend herself with and no reputation to put on the line. She had none of the arrogance that came from being trained at "the best" school. She didn't expect to be respected because of her education or her position; she was just a regular human being.

First, she talked about venture capital. In spite of the many times I'd heard it discussed at school, she took us step by step through the venture capital process, and I understood it clearly for the first time. Then she talked personally about what it was like to begin working with her current peers, previously her bosses. She admitted she had been scared to death on her first assignment. When I heard her say it, I thought, oh how can you admit it in front of all these people? But then I realized that I was so used not to admitting it at school, to putting on a good show, that my sense of what was appropriate was warped.

In comment after comment, she reacquainted me with the fact that you can be human, show it, and still command power, a most positive kind of power. When her talk was over an hour and a half later, I wanted to rush up and thank her but couldn't get near her because there were two men I recognized from school, dressed up in interview clothes, probably waiting to talk to her about jobs they wanted at TA. They looked like sharks after blood, and I turned away to head back home. I envied the women at Simmons for their program and appreciated the chance to get back in touch with myself.

I was flying high for a few days. It took the Investment Management exam to bring me down. And the crash was quick and painful. I had studied hard for the exam, days and nights dedicated to reviewing bond- and stock-valuation methods and other esoterics. For the exam Kate and I sat next to each other, hoping our minds would form a collective pool of wisdom. We looked at each other often during the four hours; by now we could read each other's stress signals. Kate's face was flushed red and her back was wet with sweat. I bit every fingernail. When we came out of the exam it was snowing, but I didn't put the hood up on my jacket. I didn't care whether I was cold and wet because I was serenely numb.

We were whipped pups. Kate said Gabriel Doucette knew it.

"Every time I looked up he was looking at us," she said. "He could see the steam rising from our corner of the room. Did you know that I ate three apples and a half pound of peanuts? I needed all the energy I could get."

"It didn't do me any good to have all of my notes there," I replied. "I was so unnerved by that options question I almost gave up and didn't write anything. We looped again, sport."

The exam was brutal and even now I don't think I understand the questions enough to repeat them—neither had any resemblance to anything we had learned in class.

I churned through my other exams. My schedule wasn't as easy as last year's, when I had had one a day. This year I had four exams in two days, which meant eight hours of tests each day. I did the best I could and went off to Christmas vacation feeling exhausted but triumphant—only one semester to go!

By mid-January I was two weeks into six new courses. I was taking Consumer Marketing; Corporate Financial Management; Power and Influence; the Business Administrator and Government; Law and the Corporate Manager; and Analysis of Corporate Financial Reports. It would be another hard semester, but at least I no longer doubted getting through and graduating. My schedule was not typical of other students in second year, for most did Independent Study to fulfill part of their requirements. I preferred to take courses, because I already had experience as a consultant and I preferred learning from Harvard's professors while I had the opportunity.

In the third week of January, grades for first semester arrived in our boxes. I yelled to Kate to get hers as I looked inside my envelope. Straight Sats, except one. I had looped

Business Policy. I was pleased with myself for getting Sats in Capital Markets and Investment Management—I hadn't a clue as to how I had gotten a Sat when I hadn't understood the IM exam. But I knew why I had looped BP. I never took it very seriously. Our professor didn't listen to what students said—he had his own agenda, and I was bored and didn't listen. Even our ethics discussion was thin and unsatisfying. I had to laugh, though; I had looped the only class that dealt with moral questions. This wasn't my strategic loop, it was my lazy loop, I decided.

Kate was also pleased with her Investment Management grade. We were definitely over the top of the mountain now and only had to hold on a little bit more and we'd be through. I knew this was so and yet I dreamed about Investment Management that night. In my dream I was sitting in class for the second time. Gabriel Doucette was the only one who knew I was taking his course over because I hadn't gotten it the first time. He walked up to my desk on the first day of class and asked me to open. The case involved the question of valuing an option, the one on our exam. All I had in front of me were drawings and poems. I woke up in total terror, my armpits wet, my body shaking, my hair on end.

It was scary that Harvard still had this power to terrify me.

8

CAREER CHOICES

February, second year. This month is what it's all about for most students. It is recruiting season and we have the chance to cash in on our business-school ticket. For the next eight weeks we have Fridays off, so that students can fly around the country, interviewing with prospective employers. There is none of the concern we had last year about missing classes. Students come and go freely during class in order to fit into the interviewing schedule set up by the Office for Career Development.

The process goes something like this. The Office for Career Development, or OCD, has sent us a newsletter each week since the first week of classes in September. In it, OCD lists companies that have notified OCD of a job opening. Students who are interested in a particular company write to them, if the companies request such an introductory letter, or sign up to be placed on the interview schedule. During this time students research prospective companies at the Cole

Room, the Career Resources Center; this library is chock-full of annual reports, clippings, microfilm reports, and reference documents. By January most of us have done our research and thus are ready for the companies that come to campus to interview. Students sign up for companies according to their priorities; in 1982 they averaged 13.3 interviews and 4.4 offers per student.

Of course, outside of the OCD process students research and contact as many companies as they want. And a number decide before February which company they want because they may have worked for them before Harvard or during the summer and like the offer of employment they've been given. But at least half of the students go through OCD, interview in January, and travel in February. In 1982, 323 companies recuited at Harvard and students accepted offers with a salary range of $15,000 to $85,000 a year.

Watching people dress up and interview has been fun, if not a little schizophrenic. By now, not many students care what they look like in class. Some have scruffy-looking faces and clothes, others don't bother to comb their hair or get the sleep out of their eyes for morning classes. I get the feeling that I'm seeing people in their true state and it makes me feel close to them, almost as though we'd all been out to an orgy together and had awakened the next morning to find ourselves smiling intimately at total strangers.

But then interviewing begins. Everyone cleans up as they did last year, only this time it's for real. New briefcases appear in class, as do pin-striped suits. Women, almost without exception, wear dark blue suits and silk blouses. They have taken to heart Molloy's formula in *Dress for Success*. Blue is the power color for women, he says, and women here don't want to take any chances.

Classroom behavior is different too. People don't slouch in their seats when they have their best suits on. When students are called on they take off their jackets and unbutton their vests as though they were making a corporate presentation. And there is an uneasy distance, another kind of competition, creeping up on us. Some people pick up their books and hurry away when class is over; they don't want anyone to ask what company they're interviewing with. Or perhaps they didn't get the interview they wanted and don't want to talk about it. Other students are just plain outrageous in the other direction. They stand up at the end of class and yell across the room to a friend, "Hey, did you hear about my offer? The one from Morgan Stanley beat the one from Rotan Mosle—it's such a deal—but I haven't decided yet; I still have to give Salomon Brothers a chance."

I can't stand people like that.

Both last year and this year I've been pleasantly removed from these goings-on. It was exciting to work with the clients of my own company last summer, and I have no wish to change my plans now. I look forward to working with Joyce when I get out of school, and I'm not tempted by anything I see to interview with companies and try to land a job. It helps to be thirty-three, I know. Again, I lean back on the experience I've had with impressive job titles and cushy salaries. Those things are not important to me; now I want flexibility to chart my own course, something that's possible when you start your own business.

Among my friends, my lack of involvement with interviewing gives me a special position. I'm no threat when it comes to talking about their plans and they feel no competition when we talk about job offers and tradeoffs. I've become "neutral territory" and I like my observer status.

But I can't say I like everything I see. First, there is discrimination, no matter what companies mean when they say they are "equal opportunity employers." I hear that it's nearly impossible to get anywhere on Wall Street if you are black or Spanish-speaking. The big firms don't like to hire these students, or if they do get in, they can expect a rough time getting promotions. Forget it completely if you are known to be homosexual; most gay or lesbian students seeking employment in any consulting companies, investment houses, or large companies would never tell anyone about their personal choices.

Then, too, consulting companies that recruit international students for their European offices won't touch the students from Asia, India, or South America. They apparently want Anglo-Saxon Continentals. Women face a similar set of problems, although in the interview process at Harvard the discrimination often seems to be more in attitude than anything overt.

Kate, Danielle, Sarah Ann, and I met late one February afternoon in Harvard Square and talked about how we were doing in our job searches. We had decided to meet for tea, but we had so much to say to one another that the tea break wasn't a long enough time to talk. We ended up staying for a beer and then dinner and coffee.

Sarah Ann had the most to say. She was doing a heavy round of interviewing in Los Angeles, Atlanta, and Boston because Jack planned to go to graduate school in September but didn't know where yet. She wanted to be able to go wherever he went to school.

"For one thing," she said, "everything they say about those goddamned blue suits is true. Do you know that I interviewed with four companies in my dark brown suit and I didn't get a call-back from any of them. Then Saturday Kate and I went shopping. We helped each other get the most conservative blue suits this side of Wall Street. I have gotten a call-back from every company I interviewed with this week and I've gotten no bullets yet!"

I was learning lots of lingo. *Call-back* was the term used

when an employer wanted to look a student over in a second interview. *Bullet* was the nickname for the letter from a company which started, "We regret to inform you, in spite of your excellent credentials . . ."

Kate laughed at Sarah Ann's tale of woe. They both told Danielle and me how hard they had shopped for blue suits. They had to do it, and yet—spending all that money just to look like everybody else. Sarah Ann bought a suit with a short jacket and a delicate lapel design. Kate bought a very classic cut. We wondered aloud how much time the men in our class spent trying to figure out whether their clothing spoke "power" or not.

We talked about the interviews that we had experienced and ones we had heard about. Sarah Ann told us of Diedre, her roommate from last year, a woman who was a CPA and who planned to work in investment banking. One big New York City bank, Sarah Ann thought it was Morgan Guaranty, had sent an older man to interview students. He looked at Diedre's background and asked if she was recently married since her name was changed and she had on a wedding ring. She replied that she was married, whereupon the banker asked how her husband would feel about her making a lot of money, which people do in investment banking, he reminded her. She didn't know how her husband felt about it, Diedre answered; the banker would have to ask her husband.

We winced. The four of us could hardly imagine the reverse situation—no banker would ever ask or even care what a male student's wife thought about anything.

"The strange thing for Diedre," Sarah Ann said, "is that the story didn't end there. The very next day she had an interview with another banking concern. This time her interviewer was not an older man but a hot-shot young turk whom the bank sent out to line up aggressive MBAs. He asked Diedre what kind of financial goals she set for her future, and when she answered that she cared as much about her working environment and the people she'd be working with as she did about the money, he exploded."

"Well, what was his problem?" Danielle asked.

"Beginning with, 'Young lady,' he gave her a lecture for the next fifteen minutes," Sarah Ann said, "about how she had to take the 'real' world seriously and how she couldn't dream of working in investment banking if she weren't more serious about money."

Sarah Ann's story reminded me of an experience my former roommate, Pat Worth, shared with me after she interviewed with a prestigious Wall Street company that rated bonds and stocks. "I happened to see Pat Worth just a few minutes after she came out of her interview. You know how composed Pat always is," I said.

Danielle, Kate, and Sarah Ann nodded in unison. Pat was always beautifully put together, and each day she looked the very picture of a young, on-the-move manager.

"Her face was red. She had taken her jacket off and sweat was running down her face. I stopped and asked her what was wrong. Can you believe this? She had just interviewed with a thoroughly obnoxious man. The very first thing he said to her after hello was: 'You know, Pat, that we analyze companies to make sure they are worth their stock price and that they can pay interest on their bonds. Can you think of any clever little tricks to help us analyze a company?'"

I looked at the three women sitting across from me. They knew Pat Worth nearly as well as I did and could imagine her interviewing with this creep. Their eyes were like circles, waiting for me to finish.

"Pat answered that she'd been a financial analyst for two years at a New York City bank; she imagined she could do very well analyzing the companies they invested in, but she didn't know what he meant when he said clever little tricks.

At that point, he started to get up from his seat. He was finished with her and the interview. 'Miss Worth, I can think of a number of clever little tricks, like sneaking into the parking lot at night and looking at what's going out on the loading dock; getting hired as an employee in quality control and finding out their weaknesses; or stealing some of their garbage to see what's going on. Obviously, you aren't the one for us,' he said."

"Obviously," Danielle said. "How awful for Pat, and what an insult to her sense of herself."

"When I saw her, she was really shaken by the expectation that she'd have to be dishonest in order to get hired and get ahead. That's not her idea of what business is all about."

Kate looked troubled. "That's what has so many of my women friends bent out of shape. They didn't expect to have to change themselves in order to get the jobs they wanted. Like Chris Cignaro. She's someone I've gotten to know from my Self-Assessment course last fall. She's another financial whiz and wanted to work in retail stock brokering. You must have heard this story, didn't you?"

We hadn't and she went on.

"Well, she interviewed with the recruiter from one of the big ones—like Smith, Barney or E. F. Hutton, I forget which. They liked her so much they brought her to New York for a second-round interview. And do you know what a vice-president asked her? 'Miss Cignaro, we like your talent, and we recognize that women have strengths men don't. We wonder, would you be willing to use your feminine wiles to win clients for the company?'"

"Oh groan," Danielle said. "What's that mean, that the company is willing to play pimp?"

Our discussion reminded me of the old madonna/whore syndrome. Many men saw women in one or the other role and either one is a tough stereotype for a woman to live down. It's hard to be yourself if someone sees you in a one-dimensional role. If your boss views you as a madonna, he can't see you in anything but the mother role, the woman on the pedestal. He would say nice things about you but never give you any responsibility, never expect you to do anything as nasty as competing and winning. If you're seen as a whore, you are the bitch, the aggressor, and you probably got where you are either because you slept your way to the top or because you ran down every man you met.

The theme of our discussion was getting me down, and it was hard to escape it. Every story seemed to have an odd twist that only a feminist perspective could untangle. But as I sat there, a fantastic science fiction image suddenly overcame me and I told my friends about it as I started to dream out loud.

"This fantasy is a play on all the times we've been seen for our sex and not for our whole selves. Imagine we are board members of an international corporation. We are in a big room, paneled with mahogany, and we are sitting in deep, plum-colored leather chairs. There are vases of flowers at each end of the room. Huge bouquets of roses, peonies, and nasturtium scent the room. There are twenty of us, nineteen of whom are women, and most of us are presidents of our own companies. The one man is the v-p for public relations and he's a very competent, though quiet man. Strange, his silences—for someone in PR.

"We all care about this firm. The success of our business is related to how well this company is doing and recently it's had its problems. We fired the president and now there are two final candidates for the position. They are men. We would have preferred women, but we are committed to hiring the best person for the job and the men are the best qualified. But one of us has a problem.

"'Oh dear,' says a director. 'Look, look at his crotch.'

"'Yes,' says another, 'just look at that crotch.'

"'How can he be head of this company? He's so small!'

"The board meeting breaks into conversation as brows wrinkle and heads nod. The directors are busy comparing crotches.

"'These men just will not do,' says the woman who presides over the board. 'We're afraid they can't face the challenge—they just look so-o frail.'"

Back in reality, we all laughed at my story. In a world of my own making I couldn't judge people on their sex, but it sure felt good to turn the tables around for a few minutes. We got up to leave and promised we'd talk again soon about our careers and interviewing. Decision time for most people was in early April, so my friends had six more weeks to experience the stress that came with choosing, and being chosen for, the right job.

I wish I could say that school was easy by March of my second year, but I still didn't find it so. True, I knew I'd earn my degree, which was why I had come to school, after all. But I also carried within me the desire to learn a lot and to do the best I could. The process of cases and classes was frustrating that desire.

Take Consumer Marketing, for example. Since my first-year response to marketing had been more panic than comfort, I still found it difficult to absorb and use the tools we were supposed to learn. Even after fifteen months of school I had the formula for breakeven analysis written in my calendar; my mind went blank if I tried to do a breakeven without looking it up. Retailing, my first-semester course, was helpful in that I felt more self-confidence about marketing strategy, but I didn't yet feel secure about the technical aspects of the subject.

I hoped Consumer Marketing would change that, and I

took it in spite of a warning by last year's students that it was just more of first-year Marketing's worst cases. The professor who taught the course, Timothy Helms, was known as a guru on the subject. Although by now I was wary of the Marketing department, I looked forward to his course. On the first day of class, he announced his intentions for the semester—we were to be prepared with good quantitative analysis every day and he would pick holes in our presentation as best he could.

Kate and I sat through the first class together. Kate was considering the course, but she wasn't sure she could take any more marketing at HBS. I was committed to taking Consumer Marketing even though the first five days in class would be spent on Kool-Aid and the next five days on a whipped margarine product. From there, the class schedule listed four days on The Skin Machine, and the rest of the schedule was similar. I couldn't expect anything different. It was only the biggest companies with large marketing budgets that could afford to hire HBS professors as consultants and thus it was not likely that we would study smaller companies and more practical products.

The first day's case asked us to recommend what General Foods should do with Kool-Aid—should it be milked as a cash cow or invested in, given new life? Halfway through class a student suggested divesting the product—to him it had lived out its usefulness.

Timothy Helms turned around and, with the strangest look on his face, said, "You mean death by heart attack, not by cancer." He laughed and the class laughed. His laugh was evil—it actually reminded me of a Dickens character in *Oliver Twist.* But worse than that was my feeling for Kate. She had just closed her notebook. I knew she wouldn't take this course from this man. Since her father had died of cancer a few years ago, she didn't find Timothy Helms very funny.

Neither did I, but I took the course and worked through case after case, even though it was almost impossible to raise my hand and talk. It was the subject matter. In my other classes I could deal with products and industries as something I should learn about. Steel and autos, oil and coal, selling clothing or stocks and bonds all seemed pretty reasonable to me. But Kool-Aid pushed me over the edge. After years of work on public policy issues and organizing campaigns in the women's movement it was rough to settle down and relate to Kool-Aid as a vehicle to learn promotion strategies or about new product introductions—it seemed so trivial.

Five classes into the course I hadn't said a word. Timothy Helms called on me to open the next day. Should Greenwood Garrity distribute its corn oil margarine in the Midwest or concentrate in its already strong East and West Coast channels? Since I had prepared the case the night before, I was ready to open and thought I did a decent job. And I found that talking in subsequent classes helped me forget my lack of interest in the products and focus on the process of learning.

Then, one month later, I was called on again to open a class on The Skin Machine—should Clairol take this unprofitable product off the drugstore shelf? I had read the case and had even taken some notes, but I never intended to present anything to anyone. Of course, Timothy Helms knew that and did it to keep the class on its toes. By calling on one student to open twice, he served notice to everyone that being called on was no gift for the rest of the semester. He did the same thing in his other class, I later found out. I was embarrassed at my lack of preparation, but even more than that, mad at the entire system.

I was mad because in the last semester second-year students were still being cold-called in five out of my six courses. It was so unnecessary for us to be under that kind of pressure when we already wanted to learn and would do the work anyway. I talked about my feelings with a professor who happened to be working on course curriculum changes. He told me that some professors at HBS believed that if we didn't have pressure we wouldn't work. He pointed out that most students reacted to the pressure during first year by working extremely hard but had the opposite reaction to it in second year. Without the threat of cold-calls they wouldn't do thorough analysis, especially in second year, when they cared most about getting jobs.

Other professors believed that the admissions office had selected highly motivated people and that pressure wasn't necessary. A battle raged continually over how much pressure HBS faculty should put on students. I told him that pressure suffocated creativity and that's what we needed more than anything when we graduated. I was afraid that I wouldn't have any left by the time I finished. The professor listened to what I had to say and I could tell he was on my side, but there wasn't much he could do to change the situation.

Aside from feeling angry, then apathetic, about the tension in classes, I was experiencing some stress symptoms I didn't much like. For the first time in my life I had a lump in my breast. When I discovered it, I dug out my old *Ms.* magazines and *Our Bodies, Ourselves* and read up on what lumps are like in women over thirty. I went to the Harvard Health Service and the doctor told me that I probably didn't have much to worry about; they were quite common in women my age. She sent me off to the surgeon's office anyway, and once there, I was told by a crusty, overworked old man that my lump was nothing, just a pea.

"Just a pea," I said. "Well a pea can do just as much damage as a baseball if it's the wrong kind of pea."

I shared my worry about my breasts with Sarah Ann. She

told me that Danielle and Sheryl Shaw had just found lumps in their breasts for the first time too.

Hearing that made me think long and hard. While we had all found out that our lumps were cysts and not of immediate concern, their appearance was still unsettling. What was going on here? Was stress causing our bodies to rebel, and if this was true, what was life going to be like once we were working and managing our careers in the "real world"? Was it worth the tradeoffs?

In second semester I had some time to think about these things. After all the reading and all the analyzing on the subject of women in corporations and women in careers, it came down every time to an individual choice: what do I do with my life and how do I do it all? Because doing it all was what women at HBS seemed to expect of themselves.

Even though I didn't plan to work in a big corporation or for a consulting firm, I had the same worries as my friends. How can I graduate from here, qualified to get on the fast track and at the same time be the person I want to be? How do I fit a relationship into my life? And what about children? If I'm on the fast track, will I have time to do the things I consider essential for inner growth: write in my journal, listen to music, and read, jog, visit with friends and strangers, and play?

My questions weighed heavily on me as I juggled what we learned from school and what I knew about myself. It didn't balance. I thought back to last fall at the end of Retailing class when our professor, Kami Ito, gave us a talk about what was important in his life. We leaned forward in our chairs, drinking his words. As a class we respected this man, and looking back, I know he was my very best professor. In his talk with us he told us to keep our sense of humor when we left Harvard and, most importantly, to turn off when we graduated.

He meant that we should turn off the need to prove ourselves. He said something else that stuck in my head uncomfortably.

Kami said he respected Harvard Business School and its traditions. And he respected the dean. John McArthur, dean of the faculty, had given his credo at a recent faculty meeting. Dean McArthur had told them he hoped to create an environment at the business school in which faculty members could teach, do research, and grow as people. McArthur had told them something about his priorities that shocked me: he wanted them to know that he put his family first, the faculty's families second, and then Harvard Business School.

Remembering that class last fall, and grappling with my future now, I thought: thanks a lot. It's great that our faculty have a growth environment. If my vote counted, I'd support it one hundred percent. But that's not what first year taught B School students. We learned that unless we worked at top speed, to the exclusion of the rest of our lives, we'd be shamed by pressure in the classroom to do more and more and more. It was an environment to be tested in, a sort of witch trial by fire, but not an environment to grow and create in.

We weren't learning how to put balance in our lives; we were getting ourselves lined up to run up the mountain, and then another mountain and another. As a woman, how could I do it? The women at school, who had the path to a successful career opened up to them, would still assume the main responsibility for family life if they chose one.

I thought of Irene Lenkowski with her two-year-old baby and suburban home outside Boston. Her husband, a graduate of the B School many years before, had recently become president of a fast moving company. He expected her to care for the baby, go to school, and have his dinner on the table at night. How could she do it all? Ironically, when Section D took a poll of what woman in the section would first be president of a Fortune 500 company, Irene was at the top of the list. She was bright, aggressive, and very goal oriented. But she still expected herself to raise her baby, tend to her home, and take care of her husband. Did she even have a chance at a Fortune 500 company?

The answer, Susan Mantero told me last year, was for every woman to have a wife. What we needed were people to help us the way men had women to help them. But I ache inside whenever I hear that from a woman. Because she didn't mean a wife, she meant a slave; someone who does our bidding, cleans up our mess. I reminded Susan of her mother, a woman who worked at home. I asked her if she realized how insulting it was to her mother for her daughter to want a wife, meaning a slave. Having a wife was not the answer.

Another alternative is to find and relate to people who want career and home life shared more equally. For a few this is a possibility. It certainly must be the way of the future. But for now, it's hard on my women friends because few men at school can relate to their aspirations or want equal relationships. Men who are headed for the top seem to want women who don't threaten their ascent, who will help them get there.

No matter what kind of face we put on in public, we were plagued by our internal doubts about whether we could be the whole and complete women we were and at the same time be ambitious, successful executives.

It was time to get the team in a huddle, and Kate, Danielle, Sarah Ann, and I agreed to meet for dinner again. By now it was late April. We had made our choices and were getting together to share war stories.

The night before our dinner I had the oddest dream. I was

taken by my Consumer Marketing professor down a long corridor that led to a room where the board of directors of Santa Fe Oil and Gas were meeting. The company was a large concern and the board members wanted to hire a financial analyst. My professor had recommended me, and on our way to the meeting, he asked about my background so that he could give me a proper introduction. I said I'd worked in the women's movement.

He stopped, turned around, and looked me straight in the eye. "Oh darn, I must have picked the wrong student," he said, "but let's go through with this anyway. By the way, Fran, these people are very sharp. They all graduated from top schools. So don't bother to say anything that isn't original. Use John Maynard Keynes as your model. If he wouldn't have said it, don't you say it."

I awoke as I sat down at their board table, and I knew I would talk even if I hadn't the foggiest notion what to say.

Kate especially loved this dream when I told it to my friends the next night. She said it reminded her of her real life interviews with the good old boys in Houston.

"'Now listen heah, deah,' they'd say—meaning of course, Girlies, you don't really belong in this nasty business of real estate development, which meant of course there was too much money to be made."

Kate was set on her plan to return to Houston and put off having children for a while. She was thirty and had a few years to play with. Right now she was torn between her favorite pastime, the theater, and her interest in real estate development. It wasn't an easy choice because although performing arts would be soul satisfying, it was a world she already knew and she wanted more of a challenge. Kate's career potential in the arts would be limited too, because she was not geographically flexible, as someone must be if he or she wants room to grow. And rooted in her decision was the fact that many people in Houston didn't take the arts seriously. She wanted, after all she'd been through, to be taken seriously.

It looked as though Sarah Ann would choose consulting because she had a chance to take her computer expertise to a firm that needed it. Danielle had thought she wanted health care administration, but her summer work experience had taught her that it wasn't as much fun as she wanted her job to be. She had just happily accepted a job in hotel management.

We talked about our other friends' choices.

"Did you know that Sally Wentworth went to General Foods?" Sarah Ann said. Sally Wentworth was a woman active in WSA, not from our section.

"Yes," I said. "She told me that the woman in charge of Pudding Pops came to school and inspired her. She thinks product management is where she'll be happiest. I respect her decision to do what makes her happy, but gee whiz, can you imagine doing Pudding Pops for your everyday intellectual sustenance?"

"You know, Fran," Danielle said, "it's not the product. It's the excitement of winning market share from your competitor. That's what makes it worthwhile."

"Even after nearly eight hundred cases, it's hard for me to relate to that," I said. "Hey, how about Carol, did she get a job yet?"

"Yes, with a smaller company in Boston," Sarah Ann said. "You remember she wanted a job in computer applications, but she got a loop in one computer-related course from this ridiculous professor—and the big firms turned her down cold in spite of her excellent background. What garbage."

We wanted to hear about everyone, but as we listened to each other's stories we became uneasy. We were measuring people, just like everybody else. The measurement process began with firms that wanted only top honors students.

Companies like McKinsey wouldn't hire Sat students. Although the registrar didn't give out grades, it was common for recruiters to ask for them, and of course, if you didn't give them, you must have something to hide and so out you were.

It was hard to be on campus without running into a dozen people who wanted to know which firms wanted you, and for students who hadn't found jobs yet it was a humiliating experience. Though we were uneasy about doing it, we couldn't help but ask about people we knew. We were intensely curious as to where people would end up.

Our conversation touched on a sore spot for me, and I thought about it for a moment as the talk continued. What was it that unnerved me as I listened to the career plans of my colleagues? It was the pressure of expectations. It came from each student and from the faculty and came in a form difficult to resist. No matter what each one of us came to school wanting to be or do, we were compelled by the relentless interviewing schedule, and by our colleagues' penetrating questions, to follow expected paths—consulting, investment banking, and marketing for the biggest companies. The system made it hard to strike out on our own and be something or someone different from the norm. And the grind of getting through school, constantly feeling as though we hadn't done enough, left us with weakened egos, unable to nurture independent thought.

I came back into our circle when Danielle mentioned a friend's name.

"You know that Jane Grant took that job with Columbia Records?" Danielle said.

"She did? Why?"

"She really wanted to go into the recording industry and she liked the company," Danielle said.

"Why shouldn't she?" Kate asked.

"Well, because the man who interviewed her kept calling her and telling her he was falling in love with her and pestering her all the while she was interviewing. What a way to start your career!"

"What a way, indeed," Kate said. "How did she handle it?"

"She didn't report him," I said. "Perhaps she should have, but she didn't want to jeopardize her chance to get the job."

Our friend's predicament reminded us of a Power and Influence class we had had that week. Sarah Ann, Kate, and I sat together in this class, and we enjoyed it because it was the only second-year class we shared. Power and Influence was a course designed to show students what aspects of their behavior they should pay attention to in order to get and hold power. Danielle didn't have the class with us, so we told her about Darlene Covel.

Darlene Covel was the president of the HBS Finance Club and had just gotten a job as an assistant to the chairman of the board of an international company. It sounded like a great job for an interesting person. Darlene was friendly, good looking, and aggressive. She wore high heels, jeans, and short fur coats when the rest of us wore down jackets and hiking boots.

The Power and Influence class focused on the topic of setting an image for yourself. Our professor asked a few students to talk about their career choices and what image they wanted to portray in their chosen company.

Darlene was the first to speak. She talked about the opportunity she had to work with this company and with this man. She didn't want the fact that she was a young woman to play a role in her effectiveness, but she was afraid it would. In the interview process, she had asked to speak to each of the company vice-presidents before she took the job. By doing that, she had established herself as a competent individual and didn't join the company looking like the chairman's girl. She told us that and then asked the class for any advice we might have on what else she could do to help build her professional image.

A man in the class offered this advice: find a guy to date in the town and be seen with him at company functions. Let people know you are involved. I thought it good advice, but it was depressing to know that Darlene Covel would have to hide herself, her femininity, her singleness, in order to command the respect she deserved.

From talking with Darlene, our class discussion moved to the day's case. It was about a young woman who wanted a promotion but who was perceived as a protégée, a "pet," of her mentor, a company principal. How does she get out of her predicament? Some students thought she should stay despite rumors and prove office gossip wrong. Some thought she should leave the company; she didn't stand a chance at being taken seriously.

I realized as I listened to the discussion that men and women are worlds apart when it comes to dealing with sexuality in the workplace. For men, anything goes. For women, nothing does. I raised my hand and told the class my view on sexual harassment and how damaging it is to women. I cited examples of how hard it was for men to even see the problem.

"On one hand, I offer you the case of a close friend in Washington, D.C. She is very capable and moving pretty fast in her agency, the Department of Energy. She was offered a prominent position in the agency if she would have an affair with her boss. She refused and instead he demoted her, a move that hurt her career since no explanation was given for his action.

"Now, on the other hand, I give you two experiences that I had last year. Somehow I got to talking about this subject over dinner with a few men from my section. One of them said he had been harassed by his boss, a woman. They had worked on a project together, so they celebrated; they got drunk and she invited him to stay the night. He refused and the next day she apologized. I protested his claim that he'd been harassed. It was a plain old proposition," I said.

"The other experience I had was entirely of my own making. It happened when Kate, Danielle, and a few women from second year and I went out on a Friday night to talk about exams.

"We were a little outrageous, shouting and singing as we crossed the bridge. I saw Woody Wade, a fellow from our section. He stood just ahead of us and he had his back to me as we walked by. I couldn't resist; I reached out and patted him on the butt.

"Well, I thought about it on the weekend, and the first thing on Monday, I apologized. I told him I was really sorry, I hadn't meant to offend him or treat him like a sex object. His buddies were in hysterics. They said I was nuts; it was the best thing that had happened to Woody all semester!"

The conclusion I drew from all of this is that men don't see themselves as vulnerable. They aren't. And they can't quite grasp, nor do they work very hard to understand, how hard it is for women to walk a fine line between being feminine, being themselves, and beating the hell out of their competition.

The class understood what I meant, I think, and so did Danielle, Kate, and Sarah Ann. Where would we find the balance to be our healthy, wholesome selves when it felt like half the world saw us as madonnas or whores?

9

GRADUATION AND AFTERTHOUGHTS

By mid-May the decisions have been made and for most of us it means packing up and moving to begin the future of our dreams. Exams for second-year students are over; graduation is three weeks away. We have some time to rest and reflect on where we're going and where we've been.

At first, in the emptiness of no classes, no cases, no pressure, I feel abandoned and wonder how I'll fill my time. Harvard has been in control of it for two years, and without the direction, I struggle to spend my days on meaningful chores. But slowly I recover my old spirit and start to write letters and read novels and spend hours walking on the beach.

I'm at a turning point in my life. Yet another, I tell myself. My God, how many are there going to be? But I can't deny it. Even though I want my own business and now head into it full time, I'm not the same go-getter I was in my twenties.

Now I want more time for me, time to appreciate and glory in living. I recall the conversation I had with the Harvard University dentist who fixed my aching tooth last year. It was in the fall of 1980, in the crush of news stories about Mary Cunningham, 1979 honors graduate from HBS.

"Hey, now don't go out and do a Mary Cunningham," he said to me.

I was stuck in his chair like a mouse trapped under a cat's paw, my mouth full of stainless steel. I couldn't reply, but shook my head vehemently, disagreeing with his implied assumptions about Cunningham's wrongdoing. I wondered if he relished this situation, and was convinced of it when he continued as though I hadn't responded at all.

"You've got drive and determination, I can see it in your eyes. You're going to go far. But don't let your emotions get the best of you."

It was a painful position to be in—not the tooth, which was anaesthetized, but the situation. I couldn't talk back.

He continued, "I know you business school students. You're out to conquer the world. Why, I'll bet when you graduate you'll have a fat job offer and earn more than forty grand."

He was pushing me past my limit. He made the mistake of leaving the office for a few seconds, and I took out the contraption that kept my mouth open wide. When he came back, I smiled and said, "I certainly hope so, Dr. Nicolli, I was making forty grand before I came to school."

He laughed and laughed and laughed. He knew I'd gotten the best of him and he loved it.

I did too, at the time, but was that the way I felt now? Now I was packing my belongings and getting ready to leave. The two-foot-high stack of cases that I'd gotten the first day of school had multiplied into six cartons, nearly fifteen feet of cases and notes. All of that information rammed through my head, and what difference did it make?

A gold earring caught my eye as I was putting things into boxes. It brought me back to the day before school started, when I arrived at Logan Airport. I'd found the earring just as I stepped off the curb and had put it in my pocket, studying it in the taxi on the way to school. It was a single earring, lost by someone with taste like my own. The shape was the Oriental symbol for balance, a gold Yin and Yang that lay in my palm like some message about my future.

I kept it on my desk for those first weeks and then moved it to my dresser top when I took an apartment. Now I've found it in a jewelry box, where I must have put it when I no longer needed to consult it on a daily basis. It represented so much—the precious balance in my life that got me through the program. I could recall staring at it at the end of the day, letting its powerful message sink into my psyche.

That message has the same effect on me now as I recognize how important balance has been in my life. The fact that I've set goals for myself, even gotten through Harvard Business School, is not the clue to my happiness or peace of mind. Much more important is the fact that I'm still myself, still know myself and still share myself with others. I can still take time to find my heart of hearts and follow it. I tuck the gold earring in my pocket and think about it as I recall what I've been through.

I could look back now and say school was worth it, but why? On the surface it was hard to see anything but pain in my last two years. Beyond the pain, though, it feels like a whole new world is opening up for me.

Years ago, working in the women's movement, I often had a fantasy of forming a network of women who are business professionals—investors, bankers, tax accountants, lawyers, computer specialists, a cadre of people interested in helping other women who wanted to grow businesses of their own. I didn't know how to do it, I simply knew it could be a success because so many women have good business ideas but lack the support system and self-confidence to carry them out.

Before school I had unformed dreams in my head, and now I can give them shape and life. Before learning all I did at Harvard, I could only guess at the contribution I could make to helping small business grow. Now I can see how Joyce and I can build our business and, as we do it, create a venture time fund, where we put our time and perhaps money into good ideas. We can trade our advice for a stake in the future profits of a company, can provide what's needed without being a drain on a firm's cash flow; then if it's successful, it can pay back our investment later.

This idea and many others bubbled up and took form as I headed toward graduation. My new sense of power over my future allowed me to focus on how I was different and what exactly I had learned in my twenty-two courses. I thought of Marketing and knew that before taking it I couldn't grasp the mechanics of selling a product; I used to make decisions on instinct and then had to live with the consequences. Now I have a set of tools, like market segmentation and product position, with which to evaluate decisions.

There are other aspects of my training that open the world to me. Before Harvard, I didn't understand what made companies grow, how they made strategy or why they made certain tradeoffs. I didn't have any conception about how the stock, bond, or money markets functioned. I didn't know how to go to a banker and ask for a loan or how to negotiate favorable terms in a deal. All of these things are now in my reach.

A recent experience made me realize that I really am different. In April, Joyce and I made a presentation about our advisory service to a bank's president, vice-presidents, and branch managers. We did it with ease and it surprised me, for two years ago I wouldn't have known what to say to these people who understood numbers so much better than I did.

And I found that the bank president, when answering my question about loan officer limits and terms, looked me straight in the eye and nodded as if I understood why his bank was insisting on its stringent requirements for small business clients. He assumed I knew the situation of banks in early 1982 and knew the effect of high interest rates on his balance sheet. I didn't mind his assumption. That was just what I wanted from school—the benefit of the doubt.

Perhaps Lisa, a friend from Section G, said it best when she described how her education gave her wings and let her do things she had never imagined for herself. She came to school at twenty-four with a master's degree in economics and a very quick mind. She leaves as product manager for a new electronic product planned by one of the fast-growth video companies. Lisa, who will probably graduate with honors, turned down offers from investment banking houses and the top consulting firms when she decided to work for her California company. By coming to Harvard, she indeed has given herself wings.

For Kate and Sarah Ann it is the same. Kate will be an acquisitions analyst for an investment company in Houston. The people she'll be working with, she says, are dynamic and flexible; they'll help her develop into the kind of financial specialist she has always dreamed of being. Before Harvard, she wouldn't have gotten past the nameplate on the door.

Sarah Ann Collins will bring computer systems into the Atlanta branch office of a consulting firm, the first woman hired for Atlanta by this well-known company. She knows it's the aura of her Harvard training that got her the job, even though she doubts she'll use the tools acquired in the process of getting her MBA for most of her work.

Dorothy Henderson also comes to mind. President of the Student Association and a likely honors graduate, Dorothy never ceases to floor me. She ran the Boston Marathon both years she was at school and polished off interviews with the dozen or so companies that pursued her. She collected impressive offers from consulting companies, but has chosen to take a position as a factory floor supervisor with a manufacturing company. She reasons that production problems and operations are going to be among the most pressing business problems of the 1980s and she wants to tackle the problem from scratch. Dorothy worked for a large Canadian oil company before school, and she said Harvard gave her a perspective on business life she never would have gotten from her insulated staff position.

Yet, with all the success, there are some who feel diminished by the experience and it would be wrong to leave them out.

"The most debilitating, regressive, exploitive educational experience I can imagine," Mary Smythe, a WSA supporter, says. Mary has exciting plans—she has accepted an offer for nearly sixty thousand dollars as the director of sales for a small company in Ohio, but she still reels from the way she felt last year. She believes that the faculty relish the power plays they pull on students, and no matter how much they protest, they supported the forced Low Pass system as a method of getting us to work harder. Mary feels, too, that business school may have been a place to shape self-confidence, but it certainly was no environment in which to build it, for there were too many times when she was made to feel bad about herself.

Although earning my MBA was worth it, I questioned whether school had to be the way it was. I could tell from my dreams that all was not well with me yet. I dreamed about courses and classes almost every night. And in nearly every dream I struggled with some humiliation or another. The morning I started to pack I awoke from a dream yelling "Taco, Taco." In my dream I was in Retailing class with Kami Ito, my favorite professor, but I'd forgotten his name and had substituted instead a favorite Mexican dinner. In calling out to him with the wrong name, I embarrassed myself and, riveted to my seat, sank as low as I could toward the floor. Kami looked at me and smiled, not angry at all.

What he didn't know in my dream, and what most professors probably don't recognize in real life, is that out of our training comes a pervasive sense of humiliation at making a mistake. Insecurity fed on fear, which then bred arrogance. It was summarized for me by a second-year professor who closed his last class of the course with a list of the mistakes MBAs most often make.

The list was an indictment of HBS, I thought, for on it were the symptoms of people trying to hide their mistakes. My professor said the graduates who failed didn't create an environment for people to work in, they were overly concerned about themselves, they believed they were more critical to an organization than support personnel, and they were arrogant and unable to take criticism gracefully. As he talked, encouraging us to be broad-minded as we approached our first jobs, I wondered if he realized how much it was Harvard's fault that we left school with those unsavory characteristics.

It seems to me that the faculty believe that the forced Low Pass system is a healthy mirror of society. They probably reason that in the business world some people fail while others succeed and that struggling to make it will force us to be more realistic business people. But if this is their reasoning, it is flawed. The best kind of educational system is one that pulls with the students, not against them. There is no need for education to be a win/lose game, because in struggling to win, we all lose sight of what we came to school for: simply to be good managers.

For this reason, it is no surprise to read the current criticism of MBAs in newspapers and magazines. We prefer staff roles; we only look out for number one; we understand finance, not people; we are callous. These are some of the problems with MBAs that head most complaint lists. These complaints are valid because of our sterile training, our lack of capacity to deal with human empathy or love. We give back to the world the values we are taught at school, values supported by the biggest businesses we read about each day. We can't learn to utilize "quality control circles" and employ human relations skills when the process of gaining our MBA skills is so dehumanizing.

Somehow, the school knows all of this but cannot bring itself to change. Part of the blame must be placed on company representatives who come to recruit at Harvard. They want to see the school as tough and knuckle-crunching as its reputation. We were routinely encouraged by the Office for Career Development to tone down our response to the recruiters' inevitable question about how school is going.

"Tell them it is fine," OCD said. "Remember they've been out of school for a while themselves and probably are nostalgic about it if they graduated from HBS. They forget all the horror stories and don't want to hear yours."

I think that advice deadly, for it robs us of the ability to see our education for what it is.

The school can't see its own problems for other reasons, too. The students themselves are a formidable obstacle. When in 1982 the faculty voted unanimously to ease the first- and second-year work load to allow for more reflection on cases, some second-year students were horrified. They felt the degrees they would earn in June were devalued in the process. If they had done it, so could others. What crap! With such reasoning, how can the human race make any progress?

The greatest source of difficulty rests with the school. It has been and is still considered to be the predominant influence on business education. It is therefore hard to challenge the assumptions on which the school is founded, but they are no longer as relevant as they were when the United States was guided by its military prowess. Now we need people who understand negotiation and motivation and how to get things done without beating someone over the head.

Like an artist who won't give up a strange neurotic habit, thinking that his or her art is wrapped up in a ritual, HBS moves on, accepting and rejecting students, letting some hit the screen and fail. It could experiment with a section where the screen wasn't a threat and study the effect on the professors and students. The results, in the 1980s, might surprise them.

The professors might then get something I couldn't give at the end of my first year. I'm sad as I discover, in packing, a sheaf of letters I wrote to my professors last year. Ten of them, neat as a pin, ready to send. In each one, I said thank you for the hard work each of them had put into their course with me. I said I appreciated their efforts on my behalf. But I didn't send them because I was so exhausted by the process of going to school that I didn't feel appreciative by the time the school year ended. I no longer wanted to say thank you.

At the same time, I came across a poem I wrote to an especially respected second-year professor. Looking back, it is easy to say now that I felt the same way about many others:

Such a fine teacher
Even stones before silent
Turn gently to speak.

Graduation Day is stunning: beautiful, warm, breezy. People say that it never rains for Harvard graduations and I'm glad that tradition holds up for another year. I'm heady with excitement as people gather round to celebrate our accomplishments. As all the sections sit together for graduation, I have time to chat with old friends.

They have already discovered something I fear is true. People out in the "real" world have their own set of expectations about Harvard MBAs and even though we may not want to personify someone else's stereotype, we cannot easily escape the stamp of it. I tell Michael Mitchell about my experience shopping for a computer in Cambridge.

I had walked into a store on Massachusetts Avenue and asked a few questions comparing an Apple to the new IBM. My questions weren't that sophisticated, because there was a lot I still didn't understand about computers. The salesman asked where I worked and I told him I was in school. He asked where, and when I told him, he burst into a speech about how useful computers are at the B School—his wife was a first year, it turns out, and he sat me down, whipped up a discounted cash flow on Visicalc and a decision tree straight out of my Managerial Economics nightmares. I tried to tell him to go a little slower, but he couldn't hear me for pushing all the buttons he was eager to impress me with. I left feeling drained and wiser about who I would tell about my degree.

Michael has had a similar experience, and he tells me about it as we melt under the June sun, listening with half an ear to the proceedings. It seems so many people he has run into automatically think he knows everything about business that he's scared to death he won't have time to be dumb and get to learn a business before he has to prove himself.

"I was hoping," he says, "to have Harvard behind me and to zone out for a while—you know what I mean, live a life straight out of John Denver's greatest hits. But it won't be that way. I'm on a fast track now and I hope the train I'm on is headed in the right direction."

I tell him about my favorite comment, the one where someone listens to something I say and remarks, "Boy, you must have learned that at Harvard."

Well, no, I try to tell the person. I knew that before school. That gesture, that wisecrack, was part of me before I ever graced those hallowed halls. But people look at me with a twinkle. They know all about it, their look tells me, and I know they won't believe me. If I tell them how hard it was, they smile and cite the statistics about how much we earn when we graduate and laugh about how rough it must be in my shoes.

It's finally time to get our degrees, and Section D rises in unison. I find out that George Cohen, Michael Mitchell, and Stan Hooper are Baker Scholars. Pat Worth and Sheryl Shaw have earned honors, along with a few other students. Three out of my study group, I say to myself—wow; the old memory haunts and I remember how tough it was to feel as if I contributed.

As I get my degree, I swell with pride. I didn't think I would feel this way, but I do. The past is forgotten for the moment, my future is a golden rainbow.

My unconscious won't be repressed, however. After the partying is over, I head off to sleep and dream about being at graduation with my black gown and cap, holding a baby in my arms. The baby spits up on my gown. Lovely goo right on my shoulder. I wonder how I'm supposed to graduate with everyone when I'm holding this baby. As I wake up, I wonder whether my dream is a signal that I fear children will upset my career plans and if it's the Harvard part of me that worries about it.

We are now, by August, a few months graduated and Kate, Sarah Ann, and I get on the phone together to talk. Kate is ready to start her job, excited at the career laid out ahead of her. But then she hasn't begun yet.

Sarah Ann is more realistic. She started three weeks ago and has had a few patience-testers already. We laugh at her latest story in the string of I-thought-an-MBA-was-the-answer tales. We resolve to meet for a weekend of mutual support and sharing sometime in the fall, if we can wait that long.

It seems that Sarah Ann went to get a physical from a local doctor before starting work. He was a nice man, a real southern gentleman. Then he looked at her background and the personal details about her life. He noted with interest her recent marriage to Jack.

"Well, young lady, you are in very good health," he said, "and I wish you well at the company. However, I see that you've been married just over a year. I believe it's very important for young married couples to have time together. You should sleep with your husband every night, so I hope your job doesn't require any travel."

Sarah Ann didn't have the heart to tell him her job was almost all travel—Jack was busy with school this year anyway.

We joked around some more, hiding the nervous tension in our voices.

"MBAs and support systems aside, team," I said, "we definitely need the Equal Rights Amendment. Even the Harvard Business School can't give us that."